Cohabitation among Students in Higher-Learning Institutions in Tanzania

Cohabitation among Students in Higher-Learning Institutions in Tanzania

Its Effects to Academic Performance

Elia Shabani Mligo
and
Jael Omanga Otieno

RESOURCE *Publications* • Eugene, Oregon

COHABITATION AMONG STUDENTS IN HIGHER-LEARNING INSTITUTIONS IN TANZANIA
Its Effects to Academic Performance

Copyright © 2018 Elia Shabani Mligo and Jael Omanga Otieno. All rights reserved. Except for brief quotations in critical publications or reviews, no part of this book may be reproduced in any manner without prior written permission from the publisher. Write: Permissions, Wipf and Stock Publishers, 199 W. 8th Ave., Suite 3, Eugene, OR 97401.

Resource Publications
An Imprint of Wipf and Stock Publishers
199 W. 8th Ave., Suite 3
Eugene, OR 97401

www.wipfandstock.com

PAPERBACK ISBN: 978-1-5326-4468-9
HARDCOVER ISBN: 978-1-5326-4469-6
EBOOK ISBN: 978-1-5326-4470-2

Manufactured in the U.S.A.

Dedication

To our parents, the late Mr. and Mrs. Shabani Mligo (Elia), and Mr. and Mrs. Otieno (Jael), for their lovely care of us as from childhood to the time we could manage for ourselves; we can imagine the challenges they endured!

Contents

Acknowledgements | ix
List of Tables | xi
List of Acronyms | xii

1.0 **Introduction** | 1
    1.1 Overview of the Concept of Cohabitation
    1.2 Problem, Objectives and Questions
    1.3 Significance of the Study
    1.4 Research Questions
    1.5 Limitations and Delimitations

2.0 **Background of Cohabitation in the Literatures** | 11
    2.1 Introduction
    2.2 Theoretical Perspectives on Cohabitation
        2.2.1 *The Trial Marriage Theory*
        2.2.2 *The Attachment Theory*
    2.3 Empirical Studies
        2.3.1 *Cohabitation in Western Countries*
        2.3.2 *Cohabitation in Tanzania and Other African Countries*
    2.4 Factors for Cohabitation among Students
    2.5 Consequences of Cohabitation to Cohabiting students
    2.6 Cohabitation and Tanzanian Policies
        2.6.1 *The HIV/AIDS Policy*
        2.6.2 *The National Youth Development Policy*

Contents

    2.6.3   The Higher-Education Policy
2.7 Conclusion

3.0 **Investigating Cohabitation Among Students: Methodological Perspectives | 33**
    3.1 Introduction
    3.2 Research Design
    3.3 Tools or Instruments
    3.4 Population and Area of Study
    3.5 Samples and Sampling
    3.6 Data Analysis and Ethical Issues
    3.7 Conclusion

4.0 **Cohabitation And Academic Performance: Presenting And Discussing The Findings | 41**
    4.1 Introduction
    4.2 Demographic Characteristics of Respondents
    4.3 Factors for Cohabitation
    4.4 Perception of Students on Cohabitation
    4.5 Challenges facing Cohabiting Students
    4.6 Conclusion

5.0 **Conclusion | 57**

Bibliography | 63

Acknowledgements

AT LEAST EVERYONE WHO has ever written a scholarly manuscript can agree with us that it takes energy and time to produce the final draft of a book manuscript to be submitted for publication. This is what has been the case for our task in producing this book. Without the participation of other people, it could hardly be possible to reach the stage which this book has at the moment. We owe our gratitude to all those who participated in one way or another. It is hardly possible to mention all of them here due to lack of space.

However, we mention only a few of them. First we thank the Almighty God for providing us life, health and energy to conduct research and write this book. Second, we are grateful to students and lecturers at Tumaini University Makumira, Mbeya Centre for their inputs in various discussions regarding the subject of cohabitation and the institution of marriage in relation to academic performance. Their experience mattered greatly in making this book a reality.

Third, we are indebted to Tumaini University Makumira–Mbeya Centre for facilitating the process of research. The research process was conducted under its auspice through its Research and Consultancy Unit. Fourth, we thank our beloved spouses Ester Malekano (Mligo) and Moses Nzumile (Otieno) for their love and encouragement during the research and writing processes. Their words of encouragement empowered us to endure the challenging task of the research process.

Acknowledgements

Fifth, our vote of thanks goes to the editors and typesetters of Wipf and Stock publishers for their excellent work. Their editorial and typesetting work has made the book appear as it is now. We are indebted to them a hundred times! Last, but not least, we extend our appreciation to informants of the Higher-learning institutions we collected data at Mbeya Region in Tanzania. Data were their property and had authority to withhold them. Their willingness to participate in research and release their information to us facilitated the emergence of this book. Without their data, this book could possibly not be produced in this subject matter. We wish God's blessings to whoever contributed in the process of this research in one way or another.

Tables

Table 1: Sexes of Respondents | 42
Table 2: Ages of Respondents | 43
Table 3: Respondents' Participation Frequency | 43
Table 4: Marital Statuses | 44
Table 5: Factors for Cohabitation | 44
Table 6: Perceptions of Students | 47
Table 7: Economic Challenges | 51
Table 8: Social Challenges | 53
Table 9: Psychological Effects | 54

Acronyms

HEIs	Higher-Learning Institutions
STIs	Sexually Transmitted Infections
HIV/AIDs	Human Immunodeficiency Virus/ Acquired Immune Deficiency Syndrome
TACAIDS	Tanzania Commission for AIDS
NGO	NON-Governmental Organization
HTC	HIV Testing and Counseling
NYD	National Youths Development
TUMA	Tumaini University Makumira

Chapter 1
Introduction

1.1 Overview of the Concept of Cohabitation

COHABITATION IS A RELATIONAL concept. It refers to the interaction between two people based on their own decision enhanced by various factors, including their transition to adulthood and seeking for alternative accommodation due lack of adequate accomodations in their respective higher-learning institutions. On the one hand, Svodziwa and Kurete state: "Transition to adulthood is a period of relatively abundant opportunities and individuals are likely to form their attitudes and intentions about one particular activity in explicit comparisons to the alternatives to that activity. . .. Also decisions made during the transition to adulthood have a particularly long-lasting influence on the remainder of the life course because they set individuals on paths that are sometimes difficult to change. . .."[1] On the other hand, Svodziwa and Kurete also state: "The constraint on policy framework where females cannot enter males hostels or males enter females hostels, undesirable quality of food at the institution's dining hall, inadequate meals, no entertainment, finance, souring relationships among roommates at the institution and the desire for "sexual gratification" has led to the students to

---

1. Svodziwa & Kurete, "Cohabitation among Tertiary Education Students," 139 140.

resort to alternative areas for accommodation."[2] The above quotations indicate that cohabitation, as a decision-based relationship and a resort to alternative accommodation, is a romantic relationship in nature whereby relating students decide to live together and share what they have.[3] However, this relationship can have positive or negative effects to students depending on situations. Hence, this section provides a brief overview of cohabitation and its possible effects to the lives of students in colleges and universities.

Before engaging into detailed discussion of cohabitation, we should answer this question: What is cohabitation? Defining the term *cohabitation* is a difficult task because it is conceived differently in various contexts and types of people. People who practice it may have their own notion of it, and so are those who do not. However, the term cohabitation comes from two Latin words 'co' and 'habitare' whereby co means *together* and *habitare* means *dwell*.[4] Following these two words, the term has been defined in various ways by scholars. Mashau defines cohabitation as a consensual relationship between a man and a woman which leads them to having sexual intercourse without having official marriage. It is an intimate sexual union between two couples who are not officially married but share the same house for a sustained amount of time.[5] According to Abebe,

> Cohabitation is defined as an arrangement where two people who are not married but having an emotionally intimate and sexual relationship with each other decide to live together. . . . [It is] an intimate sexual union between two couples who are not married sharing the same housing for a sustained amount of time."[6]

---

2. Ibid., 140; cf. Spio-kwofie, Anyobodeh & Abban, "An Assessment of the Accommodation Challenges"; Nimako & Bondinuba, "An Empirical Evaluation"; Akinpelu, "Students' Assessment of Hostel Facilities"; Hanasono & Nadler, "A Dialectical Approach."

3. Ogolsky, Lloyd & Cate, *The Developmental Course*.

4. Greenberg, et al. *Exploring the Dimension of Human Sexuality*

5. Mashau, "Cohabitation and Premarital Sex."

6. Abebe, "Factors Contributing to Cohabitation," 20; cf. Ojewola & Akinduyo, "Prevalence and Factors Responsible for Cohabitation," 650–651;

INTRODUCTION

Moreover, Mustapha, Odebode and Adegboyega define cohabitation as "the situation in which two persons of opposite sex, without being conventionally or formally wedded, reside mutually and enjoy all or some of the values of marital relationship."[7] Therefore, following the above definitions, cohabitation is a state of two individuals of opposite sex living together and having sexual relationships before conventional or official marriage. Most young adults including students from higher-learning institutions engage themselves into cohabitation. The increase in the number of cohabitation among students in higher-learning institution is mostly a result of authority's inability to provide adequate hostel accommodations to students.[8]

Cohabitation is an illegal kind of relationship; it has highly replaced marriage and declined the status of marriage in society. It is mostly because of the decline in moral values in the generation of science and technology. However, scholars differ in perception in regard to the phenomenon of cohabitation. Though scholars differ in their perceptions on cohabitation—some encourage while others discourage it—students in higher-learning institutions highly engage into it due to factors such as financial problems, lack of accommodation, peer pressures, and the search for social companionship. However, during cohabitation, they normally pass through a lot of challenges which contribute to the decline in their performance.

Another aspect regarding the concept of cohabitation is its background. According to Kombo and Tromp, stating the background of the study is stating the setting of that study. It is providing a brief overview of the problem the researcher aspires to tackle and its overarching context.[9] Kothari argues that at this stage of

---

Muriithi-Kabaria, "Factors that contribute to Prevalence," 10; Eriksen, "Unmarried Cohabitation," 5–6.

7. Mustapha, Odebode & Adegboyega, "Impact of Premarital Cohabitation," 112.

8. Arisukwu, "Cohabitation among University of Ibadan Undergraduate Students."

9. Kombo & Tromp, Proposal *and Thesis Writing*.

study the problem may be stated in a general way and then the ambiguities, if any, relating to the problem to be resolved.[10] Therefore, the background of the study enables the researcher to briefly explain the relevance of the study to society.

Cohabitation among African youth is at crucial stage since the majority of them prefer sex before marriage. They believe that it confirms their freedom.[11] Thornton et al explain that parental influence contributes to cohabitation whereby parents bestow to their offspring a rich of inheritance of genes and physical characteristics that influence their children's own approach to courtship, cohabitation, marriage and childbearing.[12] On the other hand, the increase in population of students in higher-learning institutions and the inability of the government to adequately provide the required social infrastructure such as hostels of higher-learning institutions in African countries has led to risky coping mechanism among students, which is campus marriage-like relationships.[13]

Hadari and Thornton et al. explain that most young adults decide to cohabitate because they are freely living away from their parents and other family members especially during studies. They choose to engage into sexual relationships and stay together as husband and wife.[14] Moreover, Greenberge et al explain that cohabitation among youth is due to availability of effective contraceptives such as pills, injections and the use of condoms. Contraceptives encourage them to practice sex freely believing that they will not be at risk of getting unwanted pregnancies and contracting sexually transmitted diseases without being informed that those contraceptives still have negative effects to them.[15]

The act of cohabitation among students in higher-learninginstitution attains consequences which are inevitable. Mashau

10. Kothari, *Research Methodology*.
11. Mashau, "Cohabitation and Premarital Sex."
12. Thornton, et al., *Marriage and Cohabitation*.
13. Arisukwu, "Cohabitation among University of Ibadan Undergraduate Students."
14. Hadari, "Effects of Students" and Thornton, *Marriage and Cohabitation*.
15. Greenberg, *Exploring the Dimension of Human Sexuality*.

INTRODUCTION

argues that cohabitation among students in tertiary institutions results into unwanted pregnancies since the partners are not ready for parenting.[16] The female partner ends up performing abortion, which exposes her to the risk of death or damaged uterus.[17] Cohabitation among students leads to sexually transmitted infections since they engage into unprotected sex hence being infected by sexual transmitted diseases such as; HIV and AIDS, syphilis, gonorrhea and herpes.[18] Cohabitation among students leads to shotgun weddings whereby the cohabitants are forced to marry each other due to premarital pregnancies because of the expected baby or out of sympathy and not out of real love.[19] This act may lead to divorce at the long run as the partners forced to live together because of the child, not because of true love.

Timothy and Mlyakado argue that cohabitation among students leads to poor performance in academic matters at their learning institutions. Greater energy and interest are invested in sexual activities than on studies.[20] Most students who choose to cohabitate normally base on having sexual intercourse and concentrate more on sex than on studies. Cohabitating students, especially males, normally tend to indulge themselves into immoral behaviours including stealing and lying or other crimes in order to raise finances to keep the affairs going.[21] This is because female students like having boyfriends with money so that they can live a

---

16. Mashau, "Cohabitation and Premarital Sex." The term parenting (from Latin *parere*-to develop, to bring forth, or to develop) refers to the overall activities done by parents to their child to ensure the child's survival and development both physically and mentally. According to Owano, "physical care of the child simply includes all activities aimed at ensuring child survival by providing such necessities as food, warmth, cleanliness, sleep, and satisfactory elimination of bodily wastes. It also involves the prevention of harm through accidents or preventable diseases and provision of remedial work." (Owano, "Perception of Secondary School Students," 8).

17. Hadari, "Effects of Students' Cohabitation."

18. Ogunsula, "Premarital Behavior."

19. Mashau, "Cohabitation and Premarital Sex."

20. Mlyakardo & Timothy, "Effects of Students' Sexual Relationships ."

21. Hadari, Effects of Students' Cohabitation."

luxurious life, buy expensive clothes and cosmetics, and perform other extravagant activities like going to discotheques.

The situation stated above reminds higher-learning institutions to make sure that there is availability of accommodation for students to reduce cohabitation as students' alternative accommodations, especially among young adults. The government also should provide loans to all students giving the first priority to those who come from poor families, especially ladies. Possibly this will help to reduce cohabitation among youths in higher-learning institutions. The study aimed to create awareness to the society, government, policy makers and other stakeholders, so that they can find initiative ways to prevent cohabitation among young adult students, and create a healthy society for the coming generations.

1.2 Problem, Objectives, and Questions

According to Cresswell a statement of the problem of a particular study conveys the overall intent of a proposed study; and in a sentence or two, it sets for the intent of the study.[22] Moreover, Kombo and Tromp reveal that a statement of the problem is an issue that puzzles the researcher and makes him or her see the requirement to investigate in order to find a solution for it.[23] In this case, a statement of the problem should establish the existence of factors whose interaction results into problematic outcomes.

Cohabitation among students in higher-learning institutions is a practice which is so common to the point that it has become a causal way of campus life.[24] The government and private sectors have made great efforts in establishing higher-learning institutions in Tanzania and making sure that almost all regions have a branch. Despite all these efforts, still the institutions lack accommodations for students and there is unequal distribution of loans among students which are major factors contributing to cohabitation. The

22. Creswell, Research *Design*.
23. Kombo & Tromp, *Proposal and Thesis Writing*.
24. Hadari, "Effects of Students' Cohabitation."

problem, however, is not cohabitation itself. The problem is the outcome of cohabitation: the poor performance of students in higher-learning institutions in Tanzania as a result of their living together as husband and wife before marriage while in higher-learning institution as their alternative accommodation. This was the problem which our study focused on. The study assessed the extent at which cohabitation among students in Tanzanian higher-learning institutions take place and its effects to academic performance among those students.

1.3 Significance of the study

Significance of the study highlights the importance of the issues at hand. It highlights the solution to the problem which can influence educational theory or practices.[25] Therefore, a good highlight of significance should be specific, precise, clear, and concise, able to lead to more than one objective or question and grounded in a well established statement of the problem.

This study is significant because it contributes to the filling of some gaps in the literature on cohabitation among students in higher institution in Tanzania and other places of the world. Moreover, the study provides a base for the understanding of the various consequences from cohabitation and how the situation can be managed so that this act is worked on for the better.

Despite filling the gaps in literatures, the study is significant to educational policy-makers. Policies on students' freedom at universities should be formulated to guide the way students should live. In order for policy makers to formulate policies, there should be a though research conducted to indicate the extent of cohabitation among students and it effects to their performance. Therefore, this study is one of such possible studies for that goal.

Moreover, this study is beneficial to students in higher-learning institutions as primary interlocutors of the act of cohabitation. Through the data obtained and the suggestions provided,

---

25. Best & Kahn, *Research in Education*.

this study is expected to have a positive impact to students in the cohabitation relationships and those planning to engage in such relationships. The main task of this study to such students is to convey awareness to them in order for them to decide the way they should live in an academically orientated institution.

What were the objectives of this study? On the one hand, Kombo and Tromp tell us that objectives are intentions stated in specific terms. Research objectives outline specific goals of the study planned to achieve when completed and are usually divided into specific and general objectives.[26] It defines the contribution of the project in a bigger context thereby defining the purpose of the project. It is a goal that the project has to achieve.[27] Following the above definition of objectives, the main objective of this study was to examine the extent of cohabitation among students in higher-learning institution in Tanzania and its effect to their academic performance.

On the other hand, specific objectives are statements of precise outcome that can be measured in support of the project's general objective; it is a specific result that the project aims to achieve within a given time frame. The specific objectives of this study included the following:

- To examine the factors leading to cohabitation among students in the selected higher-learning institutions.
- To assess the challenges facing cohabiting students in the selected higher-learning institutions.
- To examine the effects of cohabitation to students' academic performance in the selected higher-learning institutions.

1.4 Research questions

According to Kombo and Tromp research questions are issues that the researcher seeks to answer. These questions guide the research

26. Kombo & Tromp, *Proposal and Thesis Writing*.
27. Baxter & Jack, "Qualitative Case Study."

Introduction

process by addressing the variables or concepts of the study.[28] Research questions narrow the purpose statement to predictions about what would be learned or question to be answered in the study.[29] Following the above description of research questions, our study addressed the following research questions to reach the objectives stated above:

1. What are the major factors that contribute to cohabitation among students in higher-learning institution?
2. What are the challenges facing students who cohabit?
3. What are the effects of cohabitation on students' academic performance?

Therefore, the whole of this study focused on finding answers to the above stated questions. The following section describes the delimitations and limitations of our study.

1.5 Delimitations and Limitations

Before addressing the delimitations and limitations of our study, it is important to provide definitions of these terms. According to Best and Khan delimitations are boundaries of the study.[30] Moreover, delimitation of the study is the extent to which the researcher intended to cover the topic; it is the geographical area where the study confined itself for particular reasons. Following this definition of delimitation, our study was confined to three selected higher-learning institutions found in Mbey City Tanzania, which are: Tumaini University Makumira Mbeya, Mzumbe University Mbeya and St. Augustine University Mbeya. These institutions were selected because they provided the findings which were expected from them and which could provide the image of characteristics of the targeted population (students of higher-learning institutions) and accomplish the targeted objectives.

28. Kombo & Tromp, *Proposal and Thesis Writing*.
29. Creswell, *Research Design*.
30. Best & Kahn, *Research in Education*.

However, limitations of the study are those conditions beyond the control of the researcher, situations that may place restrictions on the conclusions of the study and their application to other situations. Therefore, according to Best and Kahn, limitations of the study are those characteristics that influence the interpretation of the findings from research.[31]

The assessment of cohabitation among students of higher-learning institutions in Mbeya city was limited because the study dealt with personal relationships. The targeted population who were the cohabiters were not comfortable to reveal the truth about their lifestyle; hence, the study became challenging and few students were ready to respond to questions asked by researchers. However, this challenge was managed by being open to the objectives of the research and socialization. Through the two techniques, we managed to obtain the required data for our study.

---

31. Ibid.

CHAPTER 2

Background of Cohabitation in the Literatures

2.1 Introduction

AFTER INTRODUCING THE BOOK in the previous chapter, this chapter surveys the various literatures which discuss about cohabitation. According to Kumar, reviewing other people's literatures is an integral part of research process that contributes to almost every operational step.[1] Moreover, accredited scholars of research such as Kombo and Tromp, Kothari, Creswell, Mligo, and Machi and McEvoy see that reviewing literatures is an account of what has been published on a topic and is necessary for any research done.[2] Kothari adds that the review of literatures include abstracted and indexed journals and published or unpublished bibliographies, academic journals, conference proceedings, Government report books must be used depending on the nature of the problem.[3]

Creswell states that literature review helps the researcher to determine whether the topic is worth studying and provides insights into ways in which that researcher can limit the scope

---

1. Kumar, Research *Methodology*.
2. Kombo & Tromp, *Proposal and Thesis Writing;* Kothari, Kothari, *Research Methodology;* Creswell, *Research Design*; Mligo, *Introduction to Research*; Machi & McEvoy, *The Literature Review*.
3. Kothari, *Research Methodology*.

to a required area of inquiry.[4] Therefore, in order to fulfill this purpose, literature reviewed should be scholarly texts with current knowledge of the study with concrete theoretical and methodological contributions to the research problem.

Following the above opinions of scholars, this chapter surveys the concept of cohabitation as practiced in various places of the world and its effects. It discusses the other researches done, their outcomes and the contributions they make to our current research. The chapter discusses the theoretical perspective which guided the whole study and the empirical perspectives which led to the drawing of the research gap to be focused by our research. In the whole of this discussion, the chapter argues that cohabitation causes more harm to cohabiting individuals than benefit. The harms caused by cohabitation are in terms of living unhappier lives, negatively impacting their children, later contracted marriages ending in divorces leading to single parenting of children, and or, not contracting official marriages at all, having disagreements, fights and violence,[5] and experiencing more unacceptable

---

4. Creswell, Research Design.

5. The concept of violence is hard to define. However, violence is a behavior which one person imposes upon another person to cause harm, pain or injury. There are several types of violence, including physical, psychological, and verbal violence. Domestic violence is commonly reported by scholars and is done in the homes. It is defined "as physical, verbal and psychological abuse; economic abuse, intimidation, harassment, stalking, damage to property, any other abusive behaviour or controlling behaviour and entry into a person's property without their consent." (Seabi, "Marriage, Cohabitation and Domestic Violence," 5; cf. Leyaro, Selaya & Trifkovic, "Culture of Violence against Women"; Nabors, "Relationship Violence among College Students."). An example of domestic violence is reported by Mabuwa in regard to what the research by the Human Rights Watch found in the Tanzanian camps of refugees in 1998 and 1999. The Human Rights Watch reports: "we found that a significant proportion of women had experienced repeated physical assaults by their husbands or intimate partners while living as refugees in the camps. Victims had been assaults with fists, bottles, shoes, sticks and even machetes (*pangas*), and some had required hospitalization for their injuries." (Mabuwa, *Seeking Protection*, 23).

Background of Cohabitation in the Literatures

behavioral problems (e.g., alcohol abuse, aggression, women and children's abuses and depressions).[6]

2.2 Theoretical Perspectives on Cohabitation

We start the argument of the chapter by analyzing the appropriate theoretical perspectives to guide the argument of the chapter and of the book as a whole. The concept of theory has been defined differently by scholars of research. According to Mligo, a theory is "an explanation about an existing phenomenon, idea, or situation. It is a well-substantiated explanation about a phenomenon, idea or situation that researchers believe to be true. This means that a theory comprises tested hypotheses which are accepted as the bases of the explanation of that particular phenomenon, idea, or situation."[7] Neuman defines theory as "a system of interconnected abstractions or ideas that condenses and organizes knowledge about the social world. It is a compact way to think of the social world."[8] Moreover, Key as quoted in Jonker and Pennink defines a theory as "a systematic attempt to understand what is observable in the world. It creates order and logic from observable facts that appear tumultuous and disconnected."[9] Following the above definitions, this study is based on two theoretical perspectives discussed in the subsections below.

2.2.1 The Trial Marriage Theory

The first theoretical perspective employed in this study was the 'Trial Marriage theory.' The theory purports that cohabitation involves low investment and cohabiting individuals are therefore

6. Cf. Bumpass & Cherlin, "Cohabitation in Declining Rates"; Bampuss & Lu, "Trends in Cohabitation"; Wubs, et al., "Dating Violence among School Students"; Pal & Chaurasia, "Performance Analysis of Students Consuming Alcohol."
7. Mligo, *Introduction to Research Methods*, 5.
8. Neuman, *Basics of Social Research*, 24.
9. Jonker and Pennink, *The Essence of Research*, 46.

easier to terminate their relationships. Teachman, Thomas and Paasch, basing on this theoretical perspective, suggest that cohabitating partners who find they are well suited might consider entering in proper marriage, while those who find they are incompatible will end the cohabitation.[10] Trial marriage theory explains the trend of cohabitation which seems to be a probability type of marital life whereby the partners get involved into premarital relationship with the perception of testing whether they suit each other for the proper marriage.

According to Gold, several names have been provided to trial marriage relationships: prenuptial, post-engagement, testers and alternative cohabiting individuals. Prenuptial cohabitating individuals have a concrete plan for marriage but the actual date is uncertain. Post-engagement cohabiting individuals have even an agreement of a list of things to be fulfilled before entering into the official marriage: "graduation from advanced study, securing a specific employment opportunity, the discharge of financial obligations such as student loans for repayments to parents, and so on." Testers are cohabiting individuals who examine their compatibility for official marriage before they contract it.[11] Therefore, despite its name, trial marriage is a form of cohabitation whereby the cohabiting individuals have some sort of anticipation to have a future official marital relationship.

The Trial marriage theory was applied in this study because it discourages cohabitation by revealing its negativity. Cohabitation raises the risk of marriage dissolution: those who cohabit may have 'unobserved characteristics' which make them susceptible to separation such as poor relationship skills. However, Kullu and Boyle argue that by the years 1970s and 1980s there were rampant separations of cohabiting relationships due to various reasons, including women's increased recognition of their role in the labor market which led to their decreased financial dependence upon men, and the diminish in gender inequality in wages.[12] The

10. Teachman, "Premarital Sex."
11. Gold, "Typologies of Cohabitation," 316–318.
12. Kulu & Boyle, "Premarital Cohabitation," 880; cf. Becker, *A Treatise on*

Background of Cohabitation in the Literatures

decrease in financial dependence and its subsequent increase in separations among cohabiting individuals show that cohabiting relationships become stable only if there are conditions that bind the cohabiting partners together, and vice versa. It means that students at higher-learning institutions also have binding factors that make cohabitating relationships possible. Most students are involved into cohabitation due to factors such as desire for social companion, peer pressure, financial problems which bind the cohabiting students together.

One of the weaknesses of this theoretical perspective is that it overlooks the negative side of premarital relationships. Ojewola and Akinduyo state clearly that "Cohabitation among university students has led to moral decadence in the society. . . . living together and having sexual relationship without being married is a trend that has virtually eroded the level of morality among youth, particularly students of higher institutions. It has been observed that many of these students cohabiting do not necessarily get to the level of marriage after all. Many of such relationships often end abruptly."[13] This being the case, the Trial Marriage theory hardly holds any water in the current lives of students of higher-learning institutions.

Despite the above weakness, cohabitation as purported by the Trial Marriage theory has its positive side. The question of social companionship is crucial for students and any other human groups. Human beings are relational beings. They are better recognized in groups before they become individuals. Their engagement in cohabitation fulfils this more important virtue of being a human being. The theory is important to our study because it enables us to discuss the effects of cohabitation in academic performance, especially when considering its improbability of endurance. It enables us to discuss that it is most likely that when the relationship terminates or weakens is when the parties enter into confusion and lose direction in their academic affairs.

---

the Family; Mynarska & Bernardi, "Meanings and Attitudes ".

13. Ojewola and Akinduyo, "Prevalence and Factors Responsible for Cohabitation," 650 – 651.

2.2.2 The Attachment Theory

The second theoretical perspective used was the 'Attachment Theory' established by John Bowlby (1907—1990) and Mary Ainsworth (1913—1999).[14] It was formulated from sociobiology, ethology, cybernetics, behavioral theories and psychobiology to explain the emotional bonding and its anxiety, buffering and growth, promoting functions in child and childhood.[15] Bowlby and Ainsworth proposed that human infants have means of protecting themselves from physical and psychological threats, promoting their well-being, and increasing their self-efficacy. Parents provide to their infants and adolescents a 'secure base' for them to survive. A secure base "from which a child or an adolescent can make sorties into the outside world and to which he can return knowing for sure that he will be welcomed when he gets there, nourished physically and emotionally, comforted if distressed, reassured if frightened. In essence this role is one of being available, ready to respond when called upon to encourage and perhaps assist, but to intervene actively only when clearly necessary."[16] Therefore, the main goal of attachment theory is to sustain a sense of safety to the growing infant.

Bowlby describes individual differences in the system of functioning interaction with attachment-figures who are available in times of need and who are sensitive and construct positive mental representation of themselves and others.[17] As Berghaus clearly states: "Attachment theory 'rests on the concept of an 'attachment behavioral system'—a homeostatic process that regulates infant proximity-seeking and contact-maintaining behaviors with specific individuals to provide physical or psychological safety and security.'"[18] However, when attachment figures are not reliable,

---

14. Berghaus, "A New Look at Attachment Theory"; Ainsworth & Bowlby, "An Ethological Approach"; Bretherton, "The Origins of Attachment Theory."
15. Bowlby, *A Secure Base*.
16. Bowlby, *A Secure Base*, 11.
17. Bowlby, *Attachment and Loss*.
18. Berghaus, "A New Look at Attachment Theory," 6.

Background of Cohabitation in the Literatures

available and supportive, proximity seeking fails to relieve distress and negative models of self are formed; hence, the child enters into the feeling of insecure.

One of the great strengths of attachment theory is that it follows a common sense appeal in the question of parenting roles. Bowlby himself succinctly stated: "The infant and young child should experience a warm, intimate, and continuous relationship with his mother (or permanent mother substitute) in which both find satisfaction and enjoyment."[19] Moreover, the concept of the attachment-figure as a source of the child's security and nourishment has greatly been a useful construct to the current parenting roles. It justifies that attachment has to do with "human propensity to seek proximity to caregivers during moments of discomfort or stress."[20] Hence, attachment theory contributes greatly to the practical notion that positive parenting leads the interaction between parents and children to more than the envisaged secure attachment.

However, the Attachment Theory has been criticized of being too simplistic in its formulations. Berhaus states: "attachment theory really is too simple to explain adult relationships and psychopathology. Perhaps we should look to the many millions of interactions between children and their environments, including their interactions with their caregivers, to explain security and attachment, along with all of the rest of their development and behavior...."[21]

Despite the above observation, Attachment theory of Bowlby and Ainsworth is applied in our study because of its potential towards understanding the concept of cohabitation. It explains the importance and need of human beings living in secured and acceptable lifestyles. Most students in higher-learning intuitions commonly cohabitate and there are forces that drive them towards cohabitating, including those which lead them to safety socially, economically psychologically and physically. In a real sense,

19. Bowlby, "Maternal Care," 13.
20. Schmidt, "Cohabitation and Attachment Theory," n.p.
21. Berghaus, "A New Look at Attachment Theory," 9.

attachment theory reveals the importance of an individual having a partner as an attachment-figure who loves and cares for him or her. The student, as human being, requires somebody to love and escort him or her in order to nurture his or her human life. This requirement leads a student to committing oneself into relationship; however, in case of separation cohabiting students react with intense digress to the actual potential. Therefore, this theoretical perspective is a powerful tool to understand the roles of the attachment figures in student's cohabitating relationships and the reactions of the one secured and cared for in terms of academic performance.

2.3 Empirical Studies

There has been a tremendous rise in cohabitating relationships among marriageable couples throughout the world as compared to official marriage relationships. In regard to this rise in cohabitation, Martin writes thus,

> Over the . . . years cohabitation has moved from being viewed as a deviant form of union formation to the preferred social norm that precedes marriage and acts for many as a trial marriage. The dramatic change in the number of adopters over just a few decades bears this out. About 10% of marriages between 1965 and 1974 included cohabitation as a transition state. By the early 1990s, 55% of American marriages were preceded by cohabitation . . . . Internationally the developed world shows even a greater adoption of cohabitation. 77% of married couples in Australia cohabit before marriage . . . . In Norway, approximately 80% of individuals cohabit before their first marriage . . . . At the turn of the 21st century, Canada mirrored France, New Zealand, Mexico and Finland with approximately 16-18% of all current unions being in the form of non-marital cohabitation. Canada illustrates the diverse regional patterns of cohabitation in the difference between the province of Quebec and the rest of the country. In 2001, non-marital unions

in Quebec represented 29.8% of all current unions, compared to 11.7% for the rest of the country.....[22]

The above data indicate that cohabitation is not only a growing threat to official marriage relationships, but also an emerging way of life that most people would prefer to live. The following section discusses some empirical studies done in western countries in regard to the issue of cohabitation as related to the concept of marriage.

2.3.1 Cohabitation in Western Countries

In the western world, and the world as a whole, the Catholic Church made marriage a sacrament and a Canon low governing marriage.[23] Despite this institution by the Church, the literatures report that many American couples, both young and old, have been choosing to live in non-marital union as a step in the process leading to marriage or as an alternative to marriage proper.[24] Muriithi-Kabaria, taking ideas from Schwartz and Scott, writes that most people in the United States of America opt for cohabitation because of the following reasons: "loneliness, high expenses of living alone, disenchantment with traditional dating and courtship, [car of marital commitment, awareness of the high divorce rate, sexual frustration, education or career demands that preclude early marriage, strong physical attraction toward someone, being in a strong emotional relationship, desire for intimacy and sex on a regular basis, desire to experiment with a new living arrangement, desire for personal growth and example of peers."[25] However, this

---

22. Martin, "Exploring the Cohabitation Effect," 9–10.

23. Thornton, et al., *Marriage and Cohabitation*.

24. Teachman, "Premarital Sex"; Abebe, "Factors Contributing to Cohabitation," 24–25; Bianchi et al. "Gender and Time Allocation"; Suzuki, "What Leads Young Adults to Cohabitation?" Voigt, "Reconsidering the Mythical Advantages," 1069–1070; Bayer & McDodonald, "Cohabitation among Youth," 387–388; Ogolsky, Lloyd & Cate, *The Developmental Course*, 71–85; Waggoner, "Marriage is on the Decline and Cohabitation is on the Rise," 220–224.

25. Muriithi-Kabaria, "Factors that Contribute to the Prevalence and

option has had little effects to the expected marriage relationships as feared by most religious institutions.

Risman et al who did research in Boston (USA) report thus: "While there has been concern that cohabitation poses a threat to the institution of marriage, it might also be argued that cohabitation may lead to better marriages, by serving as a form of 'trial marriage' . . . .. By affording dating partners opportunities to know each other better, living together may help people to achieve more intimate relationships and to avoid marriages which are fraught with unforeseen problems. In addition, cohabitation before marriage may ease the transition to marital roles . . . .. Hence, there are a number of implications that cohabitation might have for the development of dating relationships, which have not been explored in previous research."[26] In this case, today most Americans, if not all, cohabit before official marriages.

According to Kiernan, cohabitation substitutes the official marriage and is considered as a kind of marriage on a trial basis.[27] Mashau distinguishes cohabitation into three categories: the temporary one which involves a little commitment of cohabiting partners to each other, trial marriage which is conscious entered for the purpose of preparing the cohabiting partners into official marriages, and cohabitation practiced as a substitute for an official marriage.[28] In whatever the case, one difference between the official marriage and cohabitation is stated by Abebe: "cohabitation involves no public commitment, promise and formal statement of love and responsibility while marriage is a public event that involves legal and societal responsibilities."[29] However, after the fall of communist governments many things changed in the world order. This happened during the late of 1980s and early 1990s when

---

Practice of Cohabitation," 10–11.

26. Risman, et al., "Living Together in College"; cf., Mynarska & Bernardi, "Meanings and Attitudes attached to Cohabitation"; Bampuss & Lu, "Trends in Cohabitation"; Bayer & McDonald, "Cohabitation among Youth."

27. Kiernan, *Cohabitation in Klesten Europe*.

28. Mashau, Cohabitation and Premarital Sex."

29. Abebe, "Factors Contributing to Cohabitation," 20.

Background of Cohabitation in the Literatures

Central and Eastern European countries entered into a new age whereby social freedom and less rigid rule were established for the welfare of people.[30] In countries like Canada, Sweden, Denmark, and Australia and Great Britain, the changes were more vivid. The released data from researches indicate that 12% of people age 18 and 24 are cohabitating.[31] Moreover, Di Giulio and Rosina report that "In the mid-1990s, about one in three women aged 25–29 in Sweden and Denmark was cohabiting; this compares to more than one woman in four in France, about one woman in six in Germany and the Netherlands, and less than one woman in 20 in Italy."[32]

Despite the resurgence of cohabitation throughout Europe, in Western European countries, cohabitation increased in Scandinavian countries then to other countries of Europe. Gabrielli and Vignoli report: "However, there has been a lot of cross-country variation in the intensity and the pace of the change. This process is most advanced in Nordic European countries where cohabitation is viewed as an accepted alternative to marriage and where more than half of marriages end in divorce, followed by Western, and Central and Eastern European countries. . . .."[33] This resurgence in cohabitation in Europe and the US indicates the way marriage patterns have changed in the Western world.

Cohabitation among students in higher-learning institutions in western countries is also an apparent lifestyle. It is mostly influenced by economic and cultural, alcohol abuse, boredom and peer pressures. Data from 2002 MSFG indicate that among men and women ages 22–44 in higher-learning institutions enter into cohabitation due to financial requirements believing that through cost sharing in paying rent, buying food and other requirements,

---

30. Smock, Gasper & Wyse, Heterosexual Cohabitation

31. Schaefer, *Sociology*; cf. Abebe, "Factors Contributing to Cohabitation," 23–24; Kojima, "Demographic Implications"; Granviningen, Mitchell, Wellings, Johnson, Geary, Jones, et al., "Reported Reasons for Breakdown of Marriage."

32. Di Giulio & Rosina, "Integrational Family Ties," 442.

33. Gabrielli & Vignoli, "Breaking-Down of Marriage."

their university student life will be cheap and affordable.[34] In this case, cohabitation has changed patterns of family life in America like in other Western societies.[35]

2.3.2 Cohabitation in Tanzania and in other African Countries

This section surveys studies on cohabitation relationships conducted in Tanzania and other African countries. In most African countries, the mainly practiced marital unions can be identified as follows: custom or traditional marriage, religious marriage, civil marriage, and mutual consent union or cohabitation.[36] This shows that, though not officially recognized, cohabitation is also practiced in developing countries, including Tanzania.

According to most researches done in African countries, including Nigeria and South Africa, one of the major issues in managing tertiary education is the increasing negative influences of climatic change in various physical and psychological requirements.[37] Students' hostel management, for example, is very vital in attaining quality tertiary education for sustainable development.[38] Students' pressures in regard to dwelling places during their study periods and the inability of the government to adequately provide the structure for funding of higher education in Africa have led to risky coping mechanisms among students. The constraint of hostel accommodation within the institution has led to the deviant form of cohabitation among students. Students are forced to live together as partners sharing things and ling costs in common.[39] Cohabitation has reached a point of crisis among youth who consider it as a norm because they believe it to be confirming their

---

34. Smock, Gasper & Wyse, *Heterosexual Cohabitation*.
35. Bianchi, et al., "Gender and Time Allocation."
36. Di Giulio & Rosina, "Integrational Family Ties."
37. Kheswa & Hoho, "Exploring the Factors and Effects," 292.
38. Modebelu and Chinyere, "Environmental Hazards."
39. Arisukwu, "Cohabitation among University of Ibadan Undergraduate Students"; Singh & Samara, "Early Marriage."

Background of Cohabitation in the Literatures

freedom.[40] However, cohabitation is an act which is against norms and values of African society. Most students live together and share premarital sex, which is risky and has harm since it ends them in abortion of unwanted pregnancies, and being infected by sexual transmitted diseases like syphilis among others.[41] Svodziwa and Kurete further note that the

> practice of cohabitating has serious health issue to the health students that may indulge in the use of oral contraceptive in order to avoid unwanted pregnancy that may lead to truncated educational aspirations. But when pregnancy does occur, sometimes the female student is more like to seek abortion as a way out. This practice of seeking for abortion may lead to another problem of exposing the female students to quack doctors who are not licensed practitioners. . . .. However, some students may not conduct an abortion or even have the money to execute it. This may lead to giving birth to unwanted babies that were not planned for and all the consequences that come with including a threatened academic pursuit.[42]

Being among countries in the African continent, Tanzania has several higher-learning institutions through which students extend their studies in order to achieve their career goals. Studies reveal that students' sexual relationships increase in most African educational institution including Tanzania. Timothy and Mlyakado state that in Tanzania youths who abstain from premarital sex achieve better in their studies unlike those long term academic goals which diminish and collapse relationship resulting in emotional turmoil and depression. They also add that cohabitation among student's leads to pregnancies, sexual transmitted diseases like HIV and AIDS and possible poor academic performance in examinations.[43]

    40. Mashau, "Cohabitation and Premarital Sex."
    41. Hadari, "Effects of Students' Cohabitation."
    42. Svodziwa & Kurete, Cohabitation among Tertiary Education Students," 141; Mlyakado & Timothy, "Effects of Students' Sexual Relationship."
    43. Ibid., cf. EAC/AMREF Lake Victoria (EALP) Programme, "Addressing Mobility"; Mwamwenda, "University Students' Knowledge of HIV/AIDS."

2.4 Factors for Cohabitation among Students

Cohabitation being a phenomenon pervading most higher-learning education institution in Africa has increased to the point of becoming a usual way of campus life.[44] This is because of inadequate accommodation for students which drive them to share rooms even though they are of opposite sex hence ending in cohabitation kind of life.[45] Moreover, Mashau revels that cohabitation is as a result of peer pressure among students and many students prefer sex before marriage maintaining that it confirms their freedom. Mashau's study discusses the different factors contributing to cohabitation in the South African context as follows:[46]

Publicity: African youths are exposed to sex and related matters through the modern media of communication of newspapers, television, pornographic venders, the internet, radio and various magazines, which arose their sexual emotions leading to the urge to live with sexual partners.

Peer-Pressure: Peer pressure results from fellow youth who practice cohabitation and feel proud over those who do not practice. Most youths look at their peers and give in to premarital sex in order to avoid being laughed at or being labeled negatively. In this case, most youth enter into this kind of relationship in order to receive affirmation from their peers.

Experimenting with Sex: Experimenting with sex is in the minds of most youths that they have to test their abilities to perform sex before they enter into real marriages making it to be part and parcel of their lives. This kind of thinking pushes them to engage into cohabiting relationships as their ways of testing their sexual abilities and familiarizing themselves to the marriage lives before they enter them.[47]

---

44. Hadari, Effects of Students' Cohabitation."

45. Arisukwu, "Cohabitation among University of Ibadan Undergraduate Students."

46. Mashau, "Cohabitation and Premarital Sex."

47. Cf. Mynarska & Bernardi, "Meanings and Attitudes attached to Cohabitation."

Background of Cohabitation in the Literatures

Drug and Alcohol Abuse: most students often tend to be involved in drug and alcohol abuse after being enrolled in higher-learning institutions; hence, it becomes difficult to control their sexual drives when they are under influence of drugs and alcohol. This lack of control leads them to engaging in either premarital sex or cohabitation.[48]

Fashion and Clothing: Being influenced by globalization, most female students cloth into tight fitting clothes. This makes them more willing to expose their bodies and make them vulnerable to sexual procreators that can buy them such kind of expensive clothes in order to exchange the clothes they buy them with sexual favors; hence; this kind of favors may lead into possible cohabitation.

Internet Services: Internet makes the youth have the world at their finger tips. They can watch most of what is going on in the world in computers and smart phones. The resurgence of pornographic images and sex videos in the internet makes most youth to be hooked by them, seducing them towards sexual relationships. In this kind of use of internet, most youth can possibly be attracted to having sexual partners who eventually become their cohabiting partners.

Despite Mashau's above listed issues which lead to cohabitation, Hadari also reveals that the increase in cohabitation among students in higher-learning institution is due to academic influence some students find it difficult to live as cohabiting partners because of financial or academic dependency so as to minimize the cost of living as individuals.[49] In Tanzania it has been investigated that most young students from higher-learning institutions cohabitate due to the expansion of youth focused media, the great availability of contraceptives, and the growing sense of youth culture. Another issue includes appropriate and comprehensive

---

48. Cf. Kheswa & Hoho, "Exploring the Factors and Effects"; Pal & Chaurasia, "Performance Analysis of Students Consuming Alcohol"; Grinberg, et al., "Hookah Use among Students"; Tavares, Beria & Lima, "Factors associated with Drug Use."

49. Hadari, "Effects of Students' Cohabitation."

sexual and reproductive health education, which comprises of information and services for reproductive tract infections, sexually transmitted diseases, and premarital pregnancy (adolescence in Tanzania).

Suzuki also mentions the children's early socialization with their parents as being the cause for their future cohabiting behavior. Suzuki describes the socialization theory which states that "children learn from parents about behaviors and attitudes toward family life including marriage and cohabitation. Children who grew up in an alternative family and witnessed their parents having courtship outside marriage are more likely to have more positive attitudes about nonmarital sex and cohabitation."[50] In his study among adolescents to measure the possibility of parental influence to children's cohabiting behavior, Suzuki found that more than a half of his respondents who had cohabiting parents also cohabited when they grew up.[51] This finding is also in line with the attachment theory stated above. Bowlby states that the relationships between the parent and the child are many, "One concerns the part a parent plays in influencing his child's behaviour in one direction or another and the range of techniques he uses to do so."[52] Following this finding, students in higher-learning institutions whose parents have been cohabiting are likely to adopt the cohabiting behavior from their parents and live such kind of life when they grow up. The cohabiting behavior of students is the results of the parents' behavior that influenced them during their childhood.

2.5 Consequences of Cohabitation to Cohabiting Students

Having discussed some of the factors that lead to cohabitation, this section ends the empirical review of literatures by drawing

---

50. Suzuki, "What Leads Young Adults to Cohabitation?" 5.
51. Ibid., 25.
52. Bowlby, *A Secure Base*, 12.

Background of Cohabitation in the Literatures

from Mashau's research work.[53] Cohabitating relationships among students in higher-learning institutions lead to a lot of impacts to cohabitating partners because they base on premarital sex rather than constructing a strong relationship with good aims in their future life time. Moreover, cohabitation leads to several health problems like sexually transmitted diseases (STDs) for example Acquired Immune Deficiency Syndrome (HIV/AIDs), unwanted pregnancies, unsafe abortions and maternal deaths.[54] Also cohabitating exposes students to the challenge of managing home and tolerating to live as adult couples in society though they were not prepared for such responsibility, it exposes student to sexual abuse especially girls who end up being raped by their partners.

Cohabitation also leads to exploitation in the form of finance and academic matters whereby male partners sometimes have to be compelled to assist their female partners or girlfriends with their academic works.[55] Cohabitation also leads to forced or shotgun marriages between cohabiting partners or students in case of premarital pregnancy. The birth of the expected baby will force the couple to stay together or marry each other so that they can bring up the child together as parents without having any real love between them. The born child makes marriage where in reality there is no marriage in the sense that the cohabiting partners are forced to legalize their relationships without their prior intentions.[56] Academically, cohabitation, in most cases, leads to poor academic performance because most cohabiting students loose direction on academic goals by concentrating more on love affairs.[57] Therefore the above review of various studies on cohabitation among students in higher-learning institution and youth in general indicate that there is a need to encourage more studies and recommendations be provided so that future lives of most young students be

53. Mashau, "Cohabitation and Premarital Sex."
54. Bahadur, "Premarital Sex Behaviors."
55. Arisukwu, "Cohabitation among University of Ibadan Undergraduate Students."
56. Mashau, "Cohabitation and Premarital Sex."
57. Mlyakado and Timothy, "Effect of Students' Sexual Behavior."

saved by importing the knowledge of the effects of premarital sex and cohabitation.

2.6 Cohabitation and Tanzanian Policies

After reviewing the empirical literatures in relation to cohabitation in western and African countries, this section visits some policies students in higher-learning institutions in Tanzania. The aim of this section is to situate the phenomenon of cohabitation in the context of ongoing plans of the nation. The section surveys policies on HIV/AIDS, the general youth policy, and the higher education policy.

2.6.1 The HIV/AIDS Policy

The Tanzanian nation recognizes the existence of HIV and AIDS in its community and its rapid spread through sexual relationships. In the Policy it is stated that "over 80% of HIV infection is through sexual intercourse. . ." and that "prevention of sexual transmission is the key in the control of HIV/AIDS pandemic."[58] The policy focuses on raising awareness on the risky behaviors that can lead to the contraction of HIV and other sexually transmitted diseases. Some of the issues which the policy emphasizes are: "being faithful to the same partner, practicing abstinence, correct and consistent use of condoms, voluntary counseling and testing, delaying engagement in sexual practices according to well informed individual decision."[59]

Moreover, the policy recognizes that the education sector is one of the sectors that have been greatly hit by the HIV/AIDS pandemic leading to the disruption of the quality of education being provided. The quality of education declines because the pandemic affects both teachers and students altogether. Following this awareness, the policy purports that the ministry of education, working

---

58. URT, "National Policy on HIV/AIDS," 15.
59. Ibid.

Background of Cohabitation in the Literatures

through its decentralized structures, will promote prevention and behavior change communication programmes in HIV targeted at learners and the workforce. The strategies that will be applied, according to the policy, include: Promotion of comprehensive education on HIV/AIDS, increasing awareness on HIV testing and counseling (HTC) and liaising with service providers to provide HTC for learners, encourage the learners to know their HIV status, sustaining education on defilement, rape, sexual harassment and violence among learners, promotion of safe sexual behavior among learners, provision of education on male and female condom, facilitation of access to reproductive health service centers, promotion of education on gender equality and the protection of sexual and reproductive health and rights.[60]

The implementation of the above discussed policy is done through the formulation of some organs to deal with the pandemic. One such organs is TACAIDS. TACAIDS and the ministry of Education are tasked by the policy to deal with the devastating effects of the pandemic among students and teachers in higher-learning institutions. The policy states: "The Ministries responsible for education and other public and private institutions of higher-learning education in collaboration with TACAIDS and NGO shall develop appropriate intervention strategies to accelerate AIDS information in schools."[61] The information to be accelerated includes the provision of adequate and accurate information in learning institutions about the spread and prevention of the infection by HIV. The policy purports that "HIV information should be introduced early enough so as to protect students who are not yet sexually active before they are exposed to sexual practice so as to equip the youth with knowledge and skill to themselves and others from HIV transmission. Reproduction and sexual health should be incorporated in school curricula.

However, the current HIV/AIDS policy does not state anything regarding the existence of cohabitation and the effects it has

---

60. URT, "National Policy on HIV/AIDS"; cf. Nyange, Sikira & Macha, "Gender-Based Violence."
61. Ibid., 15.

towards the spread of HIV/AIDS despite its recognition that the educational sector is mostly hit by the pandemic. Since cohabitation and premarital sex among students in higher-learning institutions are more rampant and contribute greatly to the resurgence of the pandemic, the policy could address important contributing areas in student lives.

2.6.2 The National Youth Development Policy

The second national policy we survey is the National Youth Development Policy of 2007. This policy focuses on youth development issues which include: HIV/AIDS, gender, culture and family issues. Youth development is a crosscutting issue which requires mult-sectoral approaches to effective implementation. The National Youth Development Policy will depend on successful mainstreaming of the youth development issues in ministries' policies and other stakeholders. The goal of these policies is to achieve the vision and mission. The vision is to have empowered, well-motivated and responsible youth capable of participating effectively in social, political, and economic development of the Tanzanian society. The mission is to create an enabling environment for youth empowerment and enhancement of security.[62]

Despite the clear articulation of HIV/AIDS, gender, culture and family issues, the policy hardly elaborates the issue of cohabitation and pre-marital sex among youth as being one of the factors which contribute to the decline in youth development within the country. It even hardly recognizes the effects of students' cohabiting relationships as youth and their effects to the nation's manpower to be produced after university and college studies. Since this policy concerns the youth group and its development, questions of youth relationships such as cohabitation and premarital sex could be given more attention and space to show the nation's concern to students' world.

---

62. URT, "The National Youth Development Policy."

BACKGROUND OF COHABITATION IN THE LITERATURES

2.6.3 Higher Education Policy

This policy was formulated to guide the provision of higher education with a regard to a delineation of mission, levels of institutions, curricular orientation and concentration, financing, governance, coordinating and linkage with the external world of international education. Some of the strategies set by the policy are: to provide grants and loans to qualifying needy students, to provide incentives to women students through scholarships and establishment of special funds, to enable students' hostels to be operated more commercially to avoid over-expenditures, and to encourage academic competitions among students.[63]

The policy distinguishes between university institutions from other tertiary education institutions in terms of qualifications of people recruited and the awards conferred after completion of studies. It is stated thus in the policy: "The difference between universities as institutions of higher-learning and [the] other tertiary non-university institutions of higher education shall be based on the major mission of pursuit, entry requirements and qualification, and the type and level of accredited award conferrable."[64]

This policy highlights important aspects to be fulfilled by the nation in order to guide the proper provision of quality higher-learning education. However, most of the issues stipulated concern the procedures to enhance better academic standards. Most of the ethical issues regarding the life and interactions between students and students and their teachers have been neglected. It is our opinion that education without disciplined lives of students and teachers can hardly be effective. With this conviction, we are of the opinion that the policy could do justice to education if it incorporated issues relating to ethical lives of students and teachers in higher-learning institutions, including cohabitation and premarital sex.

---

63. URT, "The National Higher Education Policy."
64. Ibid., 4.

2.7 Conclusion

This chapter aimed at surveying the existing knowledge in regard to the concept of cohabitation. Three aspects were of great concern: the theoretical perspectives surrounding the concept, the empirical studies done by other scholars in western and African countries, and some of the policies which the youth, as the larger population in higher-learning institutions, are concerned. Through this focus the foundation for the rest of the study was to be built.

According to this survey, it has been revealed that most scholars have tried to work on cohabitation according to their own contexts. However, most of them based on family in general and some dealt with adolescence premarital relationships. To some extent, their findings have greatly contributed to the reflection of cohabitation in society and how people differ in their perception. In Tanzania, particularly, very few studies have been conducted to deal with the way cohabitation affects students in higher-learning institutions, especially in terms of academic performance. Moreover, the policies have hardly dealt with the issues to guide students' lives in higher institutions. This chapter shows the need to have a more detailed study of the question of cohabitation among students because it has become something normal, yet very challenging to many youth who are practicing it.

CHAPTER 3

Investigating Cohabitation among Students

Methodological Perspective

3.1 Introduction

AFTER SURVEYING THE VARIOUS literatures to ascertain the parameters of the phenomenon of cohabitation in the previous chapter, this chapter discusses the ways in which research was done. The underpinning philosophies of how these ways function is called methodology. According to Kothari, methodology is the systematic way to solve research problems and a science of studying how research is done scientifically.[1] Following this understanding, research methodology is the guideline which the researcher applies in his or her research in order to accomplish the planned research intervention. It shows the methods which the researcher has used, the design of the collection of data, why the researcher has selected and used some and left the other methods or techniques depending on the identified research problem.

In this chapter we discuss the relevant methods or techniques applied during the study and why used such methods instead of others. Under this chapter, we will work on research design types and their importance to our research, research methods and the

---

1. Kothari, *Research Methodology*.

methods to be used, research tools or instruments, sampling design, samples and sampling techniques, and data analysis. This chapter argues that a mixed method approach to research is appropriate to examining both the experiences of students' lives in higher-learning institutions and determining the extent at which cohabitation takes place in the selected institutions of higher-learning in Tanzania.

3.2 Research Design

According to Kumar, research design is a plan structure and strategy of investigation so conceived as to obtain answers to research questions.[2] Kothari also defines research design as the arrangement of conditions for collecting and analyzing data in the manner which aims at combining relevance to the research purpose with economy in procedure. Exploratory design, for example, endows the ability to examine deeply the consciousness and feelings of individuals.[3]

Moreover, Kumar states that research design explains how the research will find answers to its research questions; it is also related to the identification and development of procedures and logistical arrangements required for the research intervention to be accomplished. During this study both qualitative and quantitative methods were applied to accomplish our research purpose. The reason for using both qualitative and quantitative was to have a better understanding of the phenomenon of cohabitation, its extent and its challenges in relation to student's academic performance in their respective higher-learning institutions.[4] Creswell reveals that in a qualitative project the author describes a research problem which can be understood by exploring a concept. The aim of using qualitative methods was to collect information

2. Kumar, *Research Methodology*.

3. Kothari, *Research Methodology*; cf. Giangreco & Taylor, "Scientifically Based Research."

4. Kumar, *Research Methodology*; cf. Denscombe, *The Good Research Guide*, 109–113.

from respondents on their attitudes and opinions in relation to cohabitation among students in higher educational institution in the selected institutions of higher-learning.[5] However, qualitative instruments were supplemented by quantitative instruments which aimed at collecting quantified data in the form of numbers to determine the extent in which cohabitation took place. In this case, by using both approaches (qualitative and quantitative), the research employed a mixed methods research design which combines the two approaches together in order to understand the research problem properly.

3.3 Research Tools or Instruments

What are research instruments and why should we use them? Creswell states that research instruments are those tools used in the data collection process on the phenomenon of the study.[6] Our study was carried out using two main instruments: interviews and questionnaires. According to Kumar, interview is any person to person interaction either face to face or otherwise between two or more individuals with a specific purpose in mind. In the interview process, the mouth is the main organ used in the interaction process.[7]

In addition, interview is a systematic way of talking and listening to people in order to collect data from those individuals; which eventually help to solve a particular research problem. In this research, we used unstructured interviews in order to easily attract participants' attention and avoid annoying them. The interviews carried out were direct contact interviews whereby we had to visit the selected institutions and meet with respondents personally. Interviews were done to each respondent personally. In doing that, we were able to discern how each respondent perceived

---

5.. Creswell, *Research Design*.
6. Creswell, *Educational Research*.
7. Cf. Mligo, *Introduction to Research Methods*; Corbetta, *Social Research*.

on cohabitation and premarital sexual relationships in the study campuses.

Despite interviews, we also used questionnaires. Kumar defines a questionnaire as a written list of questions and answers which are recorded by the researcher and sent to the respondent to read, interpret what is expected, and then write down the relevant answers.[8] Here, the main instrument is the hand which skillfully writes the questions according to the problem to be solved. In this case, a questionnaire should be as clear as possible because there is no contact between the researcher and respondents for further clarification of what is asked.

Additionally, Koul states that a questionnaire is a device of constructed questions which deal with a psychological, social, or educational topic given to an individual with the purpose of obtaining preferred answers in regard to some problems being investigated. The questions help the researcher to inquire opinions and attitudes of respondents participating in the study.[9] In our study, close-ended questionnaires were used; they were designed for the purpose of dealing with quantitative information on assessment of the extent of cohabitation among students in the selected institutions. The questionnaires contained the necessary demographic information of respondents like age, sex, marital status, education level, religious affiliation, occupation and the respective universities of the respondents despite the main issues of cohabitation. Participants were instructed within the papers how to feel the questionnaires.

3.4 Population and Area of Study

After discussing the instruments, in this section we describe the population and the area where we conducted the study. The target population is the entire group which the researcher is interested in or the researcher wishes to draw conclusion about a particular

---

8. Kumar, *Research Methodology*.
9. Koul, *Methodology of Educational Research*.

Investigating Cohabitation among Students

research phenomenon. According to Bryman, population is the entire group of people events or things of interest which the researcher wishes to investigate whereby the subject of the study will be drawn.[10] Therefore, the population is the selected number of individuals by the researcher for the purpose of conducting the study along with them being representatives of the entire population. The population targeted in our study included students from HEIs in Tanzania while drawing samples from institutions of such institutions in Mbeya City.

The study was conducted in Mbeya city which is found in the southwest Tanzania, Africa. It has five higher-learning institutions which are Teofilo Kisanji University, an institution of the Moravian Church in Tanzania, situated at Soweto suburb offering courses in theology, business, arts, sciences, journalism and educational studies, Mbeya University of Science and Technology, a public University offering degrees, and advanced diplomas in various engineering disciplines. The university is at Iyunga area. Others include Mzumbe University, a public university, situated at Forest area offering bachelor degrees and diplomas in law and business; it also provide evening classes for postgraduates. There is Tumaini University Makumira Mbeya Centre which is under the Lutheran Church in Tanzania situated at Uyole offering bachelor degrees and diplomas in education. St. Augustine university of Tanzania is under the Roman Catholic Church of Tanzania situated at Mafyat area in Mbeya City offering degree, diploma and certificate level courses. There is the Open University of Tanzania, a public institution, offering distance learning programmes in different courses and at different levels including degrees, diplomas and certificates Therefore, Mbeya city was selected because it is among Tanzania's great cities with several HEI and cohabitation being one of the greatest problems facing most young adults in these institutions.

---

10. Bryman, *Social Research Methods*.

3.5 Samples, and Sampling

After determining the population and area of study in the above section, we describe the area of study and samples where such instruments were used. According to Kothari sampling design is the technique or the procedure which the researcher adopts in selecting the samples to be investigated.[11] Moreover, Kumar highlights the type of sampling techniques used to obtain samples, which include the following: probability, non-probability and mixed sampling designs. In the probability sampling design, all members of the population are included in the list and then randomly selected and have equal chances of being selected. In the non-probability sampling not all members of the population are listed and not all have chances for selection.[12] Non-probability sampling design is whereby selection of the individuals for the sample does not give the entire individual in the population equal chance of being selected. Kumar contends that non-probability sampling designs are used when the numbers of elements in a population are either unknown or cannot be individually identified. It is sometimes called purposeful or non-random sampling whereby the sample for research is selected with a particular purpose or intention.[13] Following the above distinctions, we applied a non-random or non-probability sampling design since the target population was students selected purposefully from higher-learning institution in Mbeya city which included Tumaini University Makumira Mbeya, Mzumbe University Mbeya, and St. Augustine University Mbeya.

A sample for study was drawn from the above listed institutions. The above institutions were selected because they were located in the city context which most institutions of higher institutions in Tanzania are located. Students in these institutions came from over Tanzania and even outside of Tanzania. Moreover, all of these institutions were guided by the Tanzania Commission for Universities (TCU), a body in Tanzania to oversee the quality

11. Kothari, *Research Methodology*.
12. Kumar, *Research Methodology*.
13. Ibid.

of higher education. In that account, they were considered to be representative of most institutions of higher-learning education in terms of life carried out by students.

The sample size was determined before conducting the research proper. Kothari describes sample size as a subset of the total population which is used to give the general views of the target population.[14] Following the above procedures, a sample of 30 respondents was identified for our study, 10 were from Tumaini University Makumira-Mbeya, 10 were from Mzumbe University Mbeya, and 10 were from St. Augustine-Mbeya. All these respondents were both males and females. In our quantitative study participants were 9 (45%) male and 11 (55%) female students making a total of 20 respondents. In our qualitative study, 6 females and 4 males were involved making a total of 10 people who participated in the interviews. Since our main approach was qualitative, the sample drawn was enough to determine the extent of cohabitation and its effect to academic performance in the selected higher-learning institutions.

3.6 Data Analysis and Ethical Issues

The data which were collected from the above sample were both quantitative and qualitative. Quantitative data were analyzed using simple descriptive statistics. Using this procedure, data were sorted, edited and analyzed using a software package (Statistical Packages for Social Sciences) (SPSS). The analyzed data are presented using tables according to their frequency loadings and discussed in the following chapter. Data from qualitative interviews were analyzed descriptively. Steps to be followed during analyzing qualitative data were the following: identifying topics, clustering topics into categories, forming patterns from categories, giving explanation from the patterns and answering the research questions by using explanations. Therefore, following the above listed steps, in our analysis we identified the themes which are presented and

14. Kothari, *Research Methodology*.

discussed in relation to the findings of other scholars of marriage and marital relationships.

In order for our research to be smooth, we had to follow some ethical procedures. The first procedure was to make research clearance. In this first procedure, TUMA Mbeya was instrumental for us to obtain permissions from all responsible authorities. The second procedure was obtaining consent from research participants. Participants were informed about the objective of our study and provided consent to participate in our survey.

In our explanations to research participants, we assured them on the confidentiality of the data they provide to us and their own anonymity. In questionnaires, respondents were asked to only use codes instead of real names; and during interview sessions we assured the interviewees of the confidentiality of the data and their anonymity before starting the session. Cohen, Morrison and Manion explain this view more clearly when they say that boundaries surrounding shared secrets will be protected even though the researchers know those who provided the information.[15] The third procedure concerns the use of other people's written ideas. The ideas belonging to other people have been duly acknowledged using the referencing style as per the publisher to avoid plagiarism. In this case, our safety and the safety of the research participants have been safeguarded.

---

15. Cohen, Morrison & Manion, *Research Method in Education*.

CHAPTER 4

Cohabitation in Higher-Learning Institutions

Presenting and Discussing the Findings

> "Cohabiting has been associated with a number of problems including sexually transmitted diseases and HIV and AIDS, abortions, sexual abuse and violence, low academic performance, increased cost of medical care and unwanted pregnancies."
>
> —SVODZIWA & KURETE, "COHABITATION AMONG TERTIARY EDUCATION STUDENTS," 138.

4.1 Introduction

THE PREVIOUS CHAPTER LAID down the methods of collecting data to determine the extent and effects of cohabitation to cohabiting students. This chapter presents and discusses the obtained findings. As stated in the previous chapter, data were collected using primary data collection methods whereby interview and questionnaires were tools for data collection. A sample of thirty (30) respondents, both males and females, who were cohabiting students, were involved in the study. These were degree students from Tumaini University Makumira–Mbeya, Mzumbe University–Mbeya, and St. Augustine University–Mbeya.

Cohabitation among Students

The chapter is organized into four main sections. The first section presents the socio demographic characteristics of respondents. The second section provides information concerning factors for cohabitation among students in higher-learning institutions at the selected institutions. The third section is concerned with the extent and challenges facing cohabiting students in HEI, and the fourth part consist of the effects of cohabitation on student's academic performance. Following this synopsis, the chapter argues that the practice of cohabitation among students in higher-learning institutions at the research area has more negative effects than positive ones, especially in terms of academic performance.

4.2 Demographic Characteristics of Respondents
4.2.1 Sexes of Respondents

As discussed in the previous chapter, the respondents in the quantitative study were twenty whereby female were 11(55%), while male were 09 (45%).The demographic representation is as shown in table 1 below.

Table 1: Sexes of Respondents

		Frequency	Percent	Valid Percent	Cumulative Percent
Valid	Male	9	45.0	45.0	45.0
	Female	11	55.0	55.0	100.0
	Total	20	100.0	100.0	

Source: *Field Data, 2017*

4.2.2 Ages of Respondents

The discussion of findings to be done in the following sections cannot be effective without considering the ages of respondents. With that in mind, each questionnaire sheet required the respondent to fill in his or her age. Table 2 below categorizes the ages of respondents as per their responses to questionnaires:

Table 2: Ages of Respondents

		Frequency	Percent	Valid Percent	Cumulative Percent
Valid	from 20 to 24	13	65.0	65.0	65.0
	from 25 to 29	2	10.0	10.0	75.0
	from 30 to 34	4	20.0	20.0	95.0
	from 35 to 39	1	5.0	5.0	100.0
	Total	20	100.0	100.0	

Source: *Field Data, 2017*

4.2.3 Respondents' Participation Frequency

The study involved three universities shown in the table 3. The table presents the University and the frequency of its participation in the study as per its respondents.

Table 3: Respondents' Participation Frequency

		Frequency	Percent	Valid Percent	Cumulative Percent
Valid	Tumaini University Makumira Mbeya	10	50.0	50.0	50.0
	St. Augustine University Mbeya	5	25.0	25.0	75.0
	Mzumbe University Mbeya	5	25.0	25.0	100.0
	Total	20	100.0	100.0	

Source: *Field Data, 2017*

4.2.4 Marital Statuses of Respondents

Though this study was conducted to students, they were of different statuses. Some of them were married and others were not. The table below indicates the marital status of respondents who were involved in the study.

Table 4: Marital Statuses

		Frequency	Percent	Valid Percent	Cumulative Percent
Valid	Single	17	85.0	85.0	85.0
	Married	3	15.0	15.0	100.0
	Total	20	100.0	100.0	

Source: *Field Data 2017*

4.3 Factors for Cohabitation among Students

Table 5: Factors for Cohabitation

		Frequency	Percent	Valid Percent	Cumulative Percent
Valid	Financial problem	8	40.0	40.0	40.0
	Peer pressure	3	15.0	15.0	55.0
	Social companion	8	40.0	40.0	95.0
	All the above	1	5.0	5.0	100.0
	Total	20	100.0	100.0	

Source: *Field Data 2017*

The table above shows the results of information collected from respondents on factors contributing to cohabitation among students in the selected higher-learning institutions at the research area. The respondents of the research were 20 whereby 40% of the students commented that financial problem was the factor driving them to engage into cohabitation, 40% of students said that social companions led them to cohabitation, 15% of them said that peer pressure also drive them to cohabitation and 1% commented on all of the above. Therefore, the results show that most students in Higher Education Institutions in the research area opted to cohabitate due to financial problems. Despite the responses in the questionnaires, the interviews done also had corresponding results where most of the respondents complained about the financial issue as being the greatest cause. One male, a first year respondent reported: *"I come from a poor family and do not have a loan. My poor parents are the* ones paying for my fees and supporting me with pocket money, which is not enough to sustain me throughout the whole semester. Then, I was forced to accept to stay with my partner in order to get financial support from him." Other students complained of inadequate accommodation in university campuses. They were forced to stay off campus; however, the environment there seemed to be inconclusive because of insecurity. It was not only that, but campuses within their universities were also expensive. During interview a female, second year student stated thus:

> my university has few hostels, and are very expensive in a way that just a few students can afford to pay for the fees. We are then forced to stay off campus and there is no any security in some areas. Therefore, most students are forced to cohabitate to feel secured and share the living costs.[1]

Arisuku presents a similar view like that of the respondent above when he writes about cohabitation at the University of Ibadan in Nigeria:

> The increase in population of undergraduate students and the inability of the government to adequately provide the required infrastructures and funding of higher education has led to risky coping mechanisms among the students. Government policy on students' hostel accommodation i.e. encouraging private developers may have its good side but it has been observed that, the inability of the institutions in expanding and building new hostels has forced several students to look outward for accommodation. This constraint of hostel accommodation within the universities has led to a deviant form of cohabitation known as 'campus marriage' among students. A situation whereby students of opposite sex are forced to live together and share things in common without any traditional or legal authorization portends danger to the sanctification of the institution of marriage and family."[2]

---

1. Cf. Howard, "Not Married, but not Single."

2. Arisukwu, "Cohabitation among University of Ibadan Undergraduate Students," 185.

Cohabitation among Students

The situation in the Nigerian university context stated above has more or less no difference from that of our study area and of most universities in Tanzania. In that case, the Tanzanian government should identify such cases as students who are from poor families, especially females, should be provided loans so that they can concentrate on their studies and avoid cohabitation. Moreover, those universities with few and expensive hostel fees should find solutions for the problem so that students can be in a position of staying in campus.

Despite the above measures to counteract the cohabitation habit, we are also aware that cohabitation is a psychological act. Sexual urge drives students to live together despite the presence of hostels. A student can be driven by his or her sexual urge to have a companion for satisfying his or her sexual urge. He or she may have a room in the University hostel, being duly paid for, yet he or she lives outside university campus in cohabitation with a partner. Our study showed that cohabitation was due to the need of a social companion. Most students, including married students, preferred cohabiting so as to get a companion and satisfy their sexual desires. In the interview session, one male third year respondent said: *"I am married, however, while in university I was forced to cohabit in order to get somebody to quench my sexual desires because my wife is away and I could not manage to stay for a long time without it. ..."* Therefore, the student's response shows the question of hostels, though important, can have little help to prevent cohabitation. It also shows that even married students betray their partners while are away from them, which is a bad behavior that can ruin their families. In case the partner acquires STIs and other infections, it can spread up to the family especially the wife or husband. Apart from getting STIs, there might be unwanted pregnancies and having children out of wedlock.

Other respondents also mentioned peer-pressures whereby they argued that they were convinced by their friends to cohabit. One female, second year student stated: *"my friend lived with her boyfriend and she was the one who convinced me to have a partner. She told me the benefits of being in a relationship and I accepted."*

This shows that some students do not make their own self-decisions; they are driven by their fellows to choose directions, even destructive direction. Such students should be assisted by guidance and counseling departments during orientations so as to prevent such cases. Moreover, students themselves should be aware of their goals and aims of being to universities and have plans on how to accomplish their studies successfully.

4.4 Perception of Students on Cohabitation

In order to determine the extent at which cohabitation was prevalent, we asked respondents regarding their perception on the issue of cohabitation. Table 6 below shows students' perceptions on cohabitation. In the table, 50% perceived it positively, with the reason that they were mature human beings who required socializing, 30% perceived it as negative arguing that cohabitation was immoral and had negative impacts while the remaining 20% viewed it as something neutral with reasons that it has both advantage and disadvantage. These views were due to driving forces which led to respondents' engagement in cohabitation.

Table 6: Perceptions of Students

		Frequency	Percent	Valid Percent	Cumulative Percent
Valid	Positive	10	50.0	50.0	50.0
	Negative	4	20.0	20.0	70.0
	Neutral	6	30.0	30.0	100.0
	Total	20	100.0	100.0	

Source: *Field Data, 2017*

Table 6 above indicates that cohabitation was prevalent among students in the research area. The factors discussed in the above section, financial, peer pressure, having a partner for socialization, having someone to share living costs were internalized in the students' minds building in in an attitude. As it is shown in the responses, almost a half of the respondents had positive attitude about it.[3]

To our opinion, the cohabiting behavior of most university undergraduate students is not developed just when they arrive at the higher-learning institutions. The behavior is developed when they are in secondary schools and developed by the factors found there. This is because the sexual desires of most students in higher-learning institutions begin when they are in primary and secondary schools. Most students in primary and secondary schools are under pressures and restrictions of parents and school rules. Sexual relations among students is prohibited to secondary school students punishable by termination from school. Their engagement into sexual relationships in secondary schools is done secretly and with high precautions. However, when they reach higher-learning studies, where they are considered grown up people and are free to interact in the way they want, they misuse their freedom and engage into cohabiting relationships.

Mlyakado and Timothy in their research at eight secondary schools within two regions of Tanzania report that most students in the surveyed secondary schools engage in sexual relationships to a large extent causing them to have many problems, including the poor academic performance.[4] Quoting the words of one of their respondents who participated in a focused group discussion, Mlyakado and Timothy report:

> *There are many students who are in sexual relationship. . . it is not allowed, but you can do secretly . . . some students, when at school, concentrate on studies, but when out of here, engage in sexual activity. . . generally, sexual relationship is prohibited in schools, however, if a student can take charge of their relationship they can do. . ..*[5]

---

3. Cf. Alice & Florence, "University Students' Perception," 52–63; cf. Soboyejo, "Perception of Students on Cohabitation"; Maconochie, MacPherson & Racca, "Perceptions of Cohabitation among College Students."

4. Mlykado & Timothy, "Effect of Students' Sexual Relationship"

5. Ibid., 281; cf. Timothy, "The Influence of Sexual Activity."

Cohabitation in Higher-Learning Institutions

The respondent's words above indicate that though prohibited, sexual relationships take place in secondary schools secretly.

Reporting on the factors which make students in secondary schools engage into sexual relationships, especially to day secondary schools, the power of money and the influence of friends and peers were mentioned. We will use the responses of three students from Mlyakado and Timothy's research to illustrate this. The first student reported:

> *There are men who use their money by any means to get girls; they may send some other elder girls to convince you; they tell you 'accept him . . . he has money. . . you will enjoy it'. These people live with us in our community. These people in most cases target secondary schoolgirls. . ..*"[6]

The second student said:

> *Most students nowadays cannot abstain because of the economic situation. Young children engage in sexual intercourse in exchange for money so that they may buy 'chips' or get luxury thing like mobile phones and fashionable dresses. Schoolgirls are the worst if you compare with their counterpart-boys. . ..*"[7]

And the third student (a schoolgirl) reported:

> *If your friends are in sexual relationships they will convince you to do so. It is possible to help you find a boyfriend for sexual relationship. It is very common especially for boys to help their friends to get girls for sexual relationship and when they bring a girl in a ghetto; they lock the door and leave the two to do it. . ..*"[8]

The responses of the three students above indicate that the urge to engage into sexual relationships in higher-learning institutions starts when students are in secondary schools and continues when they enter into higher-learning institutions.[9] This situation

6. Ibid., 182; cf. Timothy, "The Influence of Sexual Activity."
7. Ibid.
8. Ibid.
9. Cf. Pham, Keenan & Han, "Evaluating Impacts"; Timothy, "The

49

calls for the need of educational policy-makers to control the sexual behavior of students in secondary schools in order to make them better students as they advance to higher-learning institutions.

4.5 Challenges facing Cohabiting Students
4.5.1 Economic Challenges

Cohabiting students face various challenges: economic, social and psychological challenges when are in relationships. In the table below we indicate the findings for economic challenges. Most students complained on over-expenditure thus: 11 (55%) respondents revealed that over-expenditure was the challenge they were facing, 9 (45%) students also revealed that cost-sharing was their challenge. Moreover, during interview almost all respondents complained on over-expenditure. However, one male second year student had these words: *"My girlfriend's expenses are so high; she can even spend Tsh 10000 a day just buying miscellaneous things."* Another female first year respondent complained: *"Unfortunately, I have a man who drinks so much; whenever we get a boom (money from the Higher Education Loan Board) he spends almost all of his money drinking alcohol. He contributes nothing. I am the one who saves money which can at least sustain us till the next boom."* This reveals that these cohabitant partners hardly value each other; they value each on him or herself. This self-centeredness leads most of the cohabiting relationships to breaking in case one of the partners reaches the limit of toleration. Moreover, it can lead to conflict between them making the relationships to be bitter pills.[10] Therefore, since these partners are just cohabiting the stated situation above shows that they cannot stay for a long time in their relationship.

Influence of Sexual Activity."

10. Cf. Van der Lippe, Voorpostel & Hewitt, "Disagreement among Cohabiting and Married Couples"; Hennon, "Conflict Management within Cohabitation"; Booth, Crouter & Clements (eds.), *Couples in Conflict*.

Table 7: Economic Challenges

		Frequency	Percent	Valid Percent	Cumulative Percent
Valid	cost sharing	9	45.0	45.0	45.0
	over expenditure	11	55.0	55.0	100.0
	Total	20	100.0	100.0	

Source; *Field data, 2017*

4.5.2 Social Challenges

We also asked questions relating to social challenges which cohabiting students faced during their cohabiting time. They had interesting responses. In the table below the results show that most cohabiting students were faced by various challenges. We probed further, on the lack of attention of studies as being one of such challenges. Results indicated that 11 (55%) students agreed that it was one of the challenges. A similar response was also seen during interview whereby respondents spoke about it. One of the female third year student reported:

> *Before having a boyfriend I used to perform well in my studies but after starting a relationship my performance has declined academically. This decline was due to lack of concentration in studies; instead, I concentrate much on things of the relationship which made me fail in my studies.*

In addition, another male third year respondent reported:

> *Having a girlfriend has contributed much on my academic failure in most cases. I miss lectures and participate less in academic issues because I spend most of my time with my girlfriend, either making love or just watching movies and chatting.*

From these responses, it is obvious that having a companion while at school contributes much to academic decline. Most students begin well when do not have companions. After engaging into premarital relationships, they lose the right direction to their study goals and aims.

It is also indicated that 5 (25%) of respondents agreed on conflict as being another challenge facing cohabiting students. The result shows that apart from being lovers cohabiting partners are also prone to conflicts between themselves due to trivial issues that differentiate them.[11] Moreover, in the interview, it was revealed that most cohabiting students fight between themselves to the extent of separating, or even getting physical injuries. This issue was also reported by one female third year students in the interview saying:

> *We normally fight almost every day because my boyfriend is not faithful to me. He sometimes comes in the room with another lady, or sleep somewhere without informing me. Moreover, his phone is full of romantic texts from different girls; and when I ask him concerning them we end up fighting.*

Therefore, this kind of relationship is dangerous; a student can be injured badly by his or her partner without the awareness of parents or guardians and in an unexpected environment.

There was a challenge of contracting STIs when couples lived in cohabiting relationships especially if one or both of them engaged in what Osuafor and Ayiga call as "sexual risky behaviors". According to Osuafor and Ayiga, sexual risky behaviors "include early age at sexual debut, having multiple sexual partners, unprotected sex with strangers, sex with partners whose STI status is unknown and when one or one's sexual partner has a STI."[12] In response to the question whether contracting STIs was one of such challenges, 3 (15%) of respondents agreed that cohabitation

---

11. Cf. Van der Lippe, Voorpostel & Hewitt, "Disagreement among Cohabiting and Married Couples"; Hennon, "Conflict Management within Cohabitation"; Booth, Crouter & Clements (eds.), *Couples in Conflict*.

12. Osuafor & Ayiga, "Risky Sexual Behaviour," 805; cf. Pulerwitz, Izazola-Licea & Gortmaker, "Extrarelational Sex among Mexican Men"; Finer, Darroch & Singh, "Sexual Partnership"; Aluzimbi, et al., "Risk Factors for Unplanned Sex."

leads to infection of STIs. This challenge was also reported by one female second year student who was free to be sincere that she was among students who, after getting into relationship, ended up having infection from her boyfriend. The student said:

> I met a nice gentleman at the university, and really I thought that he was my Mr. Right. I did not know that he had an infection of one of the deadly diseases. His outside appearance was so attractive. I accepted him and we stayed together; later I conceived. I went to prenatal clinic for testing and was found positive.

This is a very confidential part. Most cohabiting students are faced by this challenge, and are hardly open to speak it out. It seems that most students who cohabit have more than one partner and practice unsafe sex in most cases, which is indeed very risky to their lives and society. It is something which should be worked on; otherwise, a lot of youth will have miserable endings.

The remaining 1 (5%) respondent reported all the above mentioned challenges. This indicates that few partners encounter different challenges depending on how they behave themselves or how they view on each other. Social challenges are concerned with how the partners behave themselves and their view on relationship. Response results on social challenges are indicated in the table below.

Table 8: Social Challenges

		Frequency	Percent	Valid Percent	Cumulative Percent
Valid	demand attention of studies	11	55.0	55.0	55.0
	contraction of STI	3	15.0	15.0	70.0
	Conflicts	5	25.0	25.0	95.0
	all the above	1	5.0	5.0	100.0
	Total	20	100.0	100.0	

Source: *Field Data, 2017*

Cohabitating students usually get negative impacts in their relationships. The impacts can be economic, social or psychological. The study shows that most students are psychologically affected by these impacts. The table below summarizes the results obtained from the field. Among the effects obtained, academic decline is the highest of all the effects faced by cohabiting students.

Table 9: Psychological Effects

		Frequency	Percent	Valid Percent	Cumulative Percent
Valid	decline of academic perform	12	60.0	60.0	60.0
	Pregnancy	4	20.0	20.0	80.0
	transmission of STIs	2	10.0	10.0	90.0
	guilty consciousness	2	10.0	10.0	100.0
	Total	20	100.0	100.0	

Source: *Fieldwork, 2017*

As it is shown, 12 (60%) of students found themselves failing in their studies due to relationships they concentrated more than on academic issues. These were also seen from the previous comments reported by participants as most of them claimed that when they entered into relationship, they studied less and relaxed more with their partners, hence declined in performance. Females also seemed to be highly affected by the cohabiting relationships more than males. For example, when they unexpectedly became pregnant they always became confused. This is because of the illegal kind of relationship which they chose. Their boyfriends mostly denied them and some parents failed to understand them; hence, ending up being psychologically affected.[13] The above stated situation was also admitted during interview sessions where most female students painfully reported to be ruined by their boyfriends. It was reported thus by one female first year student:

---

13. Cf. Miller, "Cohabiting Men's Preferences" cf. Finer & Zolna, "Shifts in Intended and Unintended Pregnancies."

Cohabitation in Higher-Learning Institutions

> "We used to be good to each other before, but when I conceived and informed my boyfriend about it, he rejected the pregnancy saying that it does not belong to him. He chased me and told me not to mention him as the father of the child or else he will badly harm me. My parents also could not understand me, instead they said that they sent me to university to learn but not to get married; actually, I was confused to an extent of committing suicide. . .."

The above words portray what is typically referred to as gender-based violence exercised in cohabiting relationships among students. According to Mwaura, as quoted in Chitando and Chirongoma,

> "Gender-based violence refers to any harm that is perpetrated against a person as a result of the gender power inequalities that exist among males and females. It is an umbrella term covering any act of violence inflicted on a person primarily because of their gender. Gender-based violence is often a display of male power which manifests itself in various forms including physical, psychological, cultural, economic, and sexual. . .."[14]

The words of the informant above are typical indicators of the power difference between the two genders which Chitando and Chirongoma state above. The male partner assumes to have more power than the female partner.[15] Therefore, in the above incident, though the cohabiting act was partly an agreement between the cohabiting partners, yet it ends in a psychologically acute ending to one of the partners due to lack of the legal part. Cohabiting partners and students in this case, agree to live together without legalizing their relationships.

The remaining 40% of the psychological effects faced by cohabitating students include infections of STIs and guilty consciousness. Other effects are economic effects and the respondents revealed that this occurs through overspending by either one or both of the companions. This overspending leads them to the life

---

14. Chitando & Chirongoma, "Introduction: Justice not Silence," 10.
15. Cf. Pratto, Sidanius & Levin, "Social Dominance Theory."

of poverty and female partners are forced to look for other male companions who can afford to give them money, which further leads them into contracting sexually transmitted diseases. Males who like overspending always end up in immoral behaviors such as drug dealing, theft and robbery so that they can earn money. Therefore, cohabitation in universities among students should be objected or else the future of most young people will end into destruction.

4.6 Conclusion

This chapter presented and discussed data in relation to the objectives stated in chapter one of this book. The main objective of this study was to determine the extent of cohabitation among students in higher-learning institutions in Tanzania and the way it affects students' academic performance. The presented and discussed data in this chapter indicate that cohabitation is prevalent among students in the surveyed institutions. Cohabitation challenges students in their academic performance because, instead of dealing with studies, most of them deal with the challenges of cohabiting relationships which go against their initial perceptions and expectations. Despite the few benefits which students acquire from the cohabiting relationships, the psychological, economic and social challenges discussed in this chapter make students less effective in their studies as they concentrate greatly in the relationship. In this case, the findings from this chapter have indicated that cohabitation among students in higher-learning institutions in Tanzania pose more negative challenges to academic performance than positive ones.

Chapter 5
Conclusion

THIS BOOK HAS DEALT with the phenomenon of cohabitation among students in higher-learning institutions in Tanzania as one of the challenges to students' academic performance. The first objective was to examine the extent at which cohabitation is practiced in the study area and the effects which such practice has to cohabitants. The extent of cohabitation was examined by searching the attitudes of most students at the research area while the effects of cohabitation have also been studied together with the factors which make students adopt a cohabiting lifestyle.

The findings discussed above revealed that most students perceive cohabitation in a positive manner. Most youth reasoned that cohabitation was inevitable since they were grown up people and had freedom to choose the kind of life they wanted to live. However, there were those who perceived cohabitation negatively even though they were practicing it. These students were those driven into relationships due to peer-pressures or poverty. Those who perceived it neutrally were mostly married students who just required social companions for satisfying their sexual urges while their wives or husbands were away. Since those who had positive attitude on cohabitation were more than the rest of students, it was evident that students preferred cohabitating and cohabitation was prevalent

The second objective was to assess the challenges facing students who cohabit. Findings from this study revealed that most cohabiting students, especially females were highly facing social and psychological challenges as compared to their male counterparts. This was vivid that female students were always in danger of getting unplanned pregnancies; which they could either abort or remain single parents in case their male partners rejected to be concerned with the pregnancies. Male partners also seemed to get challenges in economic areas in cases when their girlfriends' demands were higher and yet had to make sure that they provide them with whatever they required in order to secure the relationships from being dropped.

The third objective was to examine the effects of cohabitation on students' academic performance. It has been noted in the above discussion that most students who cohabit are affected academically in various ways because instead of concentrating in studies they shift the attention of their minds to relationships. Looking at economic effects, for example, the study showed that cost sharing and over expenditure affected partners as most of them complained about the unequal contribution in the relationship which led them to conflicts or engaging into other immoral behaviors like prostitution, theft and alcoholism. Moreover, these cohabiting students were normally affected socially in terms of contracting STI infections, pregnancies and conflicts. These social effects led to students' failure academically.

On the basis of the above findings, this study recommends the following: first, the higher institutions owners should make sure that there are enough accommodations within the institutions so that students are secure and avoid cohabitation especially the young adults. The lack of adequate hostels and the higher prices of the available hostels make students have no alternative to make their student lives easier. As we have seen in the findings of this research, most of them opted for cohabitating relationships in order to share the living costs. Increasing the hostels and reducing the prices for students will most likely reduce the chances of opting for cohabiting relationships.

Second, higher-learning institutions should make sure that guidance and counseling departments are available and active in

Conclusion

order to assist learners psychologically. Though these units are important for students in various problems facing their student lives, they have hardly been taken into accounts. It is our opinion that establishing counseling units, with professional counselors, at higher-learning institutions will reduce cohabiting behaviors among students because students will be led to better ways of managing their student problems instead of resorting to cohabiting relationships as solutions of such problems.

Third, students should have targets and make sure that they accomplish their aims and objectives set. Moreover, they should not allow their feelings to drive them in performing immoral behaviors. They have to secure for themselves from cohabiting relationships that can bring them social, physical and psychological problems. The target of students attending higher-learning institutions is study. This is the utmost important activity. In focusing on this target, students will have to control their emotions that can lead them to engaging into risky relationships, especially cohabitation and its effects to academic performance discussed above.

Fourth, parents are required to take their roles towards knowing the study situation of their children. The discussion of findings above indicates that most students cohabit without the knowledge of their parents or guardians. When such students face problems, they end up being stranded and without directions. Some of them become pregnant without the knowledge of parents and relatives. When this happens, students decide to remain at colleges and universities during vacations until they give birth.

Ojewola and Akinduyo advise that "Parents & guardians must not only send their children . . . to school, they must visit them to know how and what they are doing in school. Some students cohabit without the knowledge of their parents because they are sure that their parents would never come to visit them in school. Some cohabit due to ignorance and inexperience, the desire to explore, and the sudden freedom is what prompt many of these students to misbehave."[1] The visits of parents or guardians at the institutions

---

1. Ojewola and Akinduyo, "Prevalence and Factors Responsible for Cohabitation," 653–654.

where their children study will help to both know their situations and provide help where is required before their children enter into such risky relationships. It will also reduce freedom for them to behave the way they like knowing that nobody among the parents or guardians will visit them.

Fifth, since this study focused only on cohabitation among students in higher-learning institutions, it is recommended that this kind of study be conducted in other tertiary institutions within Tanzania to ascertain the extent and effects of cohabitation. Conducting research on those institutions will enable researchers to compare and contrast the challenges and find better solutions which can help the upcoming youth to study and pursue their careers. For married ones, the solutions provided will help in rescuing their marriages from destruction.

In recent year, scholars have reported pressures from society in regard to the low academic performance of students in secondary and primary schools. The pressures have been directed upon the professionalism of teachers and the role they play towards students' learning. Matete, for example, reports: Communities have been demanding a greater say in how their schools are running and how teachers are performing to the extent that the local/ward council members can air out their dissatisfaction with the District Education Officer, and about head/teachers they would not like to be in their schools or districts."[2] She further reports some incidences of canning primary school teachers who underperformed done by police officers in Bukoba, the demand by parents that those teachers who underperformed should be removed from a school, and the commitment of suicide of a teacher after being dismissed by parents from a school due to poor academic performance of students.[3] All these incidences indicate the seriousness of education stakeholders to students' academic performance.

It is our contention that such seriousness should not end with primary and secondary levels of education. Rather, it should be extended to the tertiary level. Despite the examination of teachers'

2. Matete, Rose. "Teaching Professionalism," 60.
3. Ibid.

Conclusion

professionalism, as done by society in the above reported incidences, stakeholders should examine the effects of cohabitation to students' performances and plan for the ways to combat it. Indeed, romantic relationships among students, and cohabitation in particular, is a silent killer of students' and the nation's educational ambitions.

Bibliography

Abebe, Samrawit. "Factors Contributing to Cohabitation among Heterosexual Couples in Addis Ababa." M.A. Thesis, University of Addis Ababa Ethiopia, 2015.
*Adolescents in Tanzania: For Young Tanzanians Everywhere. United Nations Children Fund (*UNICEF), Dar es Salaam, 2011. Online at https://www.unicef.org/tanzania/Tanzania_adolescents_for_young_people.pdf [Retrieved 08 September, 2017].
Ainsworth, Mary D. S., and Bowlby, John. "An Ethological Approach to Personality Development." *American Psychologist* 46 (1991): 331–341.
Akinpelu, Olusegun Peter. "Students' Assessment of Hostel Facilities in the politichnic Ibadan, Ibadan Nigeria: Realities and challenges." *Research on Humanities and Social Sciences* 5:17 (2015) 74–81.
Alice, Omond W. and Florence, Kamonjo W. "University Students' Perception of Marriage Life by Gender at Egerton University, Njoro Campus, Kenya." *International Journal of Scientific Research and Innovative Technology* 2:7 (2015) 49–64.
Aluzimbi, George, Barker, Joseph, King, Rachel, Rutherford, George, Ssenkusu, John M., Lubwama, George W., Muyonga, Michael and Hladik, Wolfgang. "Risk Factors for Unplanned Sex among University Students in Kampala,Uganda: A Qualitative Study." *International Journal of Adolescence and Youth* 18:3 (2013) 191–203. Online at http://dx.doi.org/1 0.1080/02673843.2012.685947 [Accessed 31 October, 2017].
Arisukwu, C.O. "Cohabitation among University of Ibadan Undergraduate Students." *Research on Humanities and Social Sciences* 3:5 (2013) 185–192.
Azeez, Tajudeen, Taiwo, David, Mogaji-Allison, Basirat, and Bello, Azeez. "Comparative Assessment of Students' Satisfaction with Hostel Accommodation in Selected Private Universities in Ogun State, Nigeria." *European Scientific Journal* 12:32 (2016) 410–425.
Bayer, Alan E. and McDonald, Gerald W. "Cohabitation among Youth: Correlates of Support for a New American Ethic." *Youth and Society* 12: 4 (1981) 387–402.

Bibliography

Becker, G.S. *A Treatise on the Family*. Cambridge, Mass: Harvard University Press, 1981.

Bahadur G.T. "Premarital Sex Behaviors among College Youth of Kathmandu Nepal." *Kathmandu University of Medicine Journal* 11:41 (2013) 27–31.

Baxter, Pamela and Jack, Susan. "Qualitative Case Study Methodology: Study Design and Implementation of Novice Researcher." *The Qualitative Report* 13: 4 (2008) 544–559. Online at http://nsuworks.nova.edu/tqr/vol13/iss4/2 [Retrieved 16 September 2017].

Best, J. and Kahn, J. *Research in Education*. Seventh Edition. New Delhi: Prentice Hall, 2002.

Berghaus, Barry J. "A New Look at Attachment Theory and Adult 'Attachment' Behavior." *Behaviorology Today* 14:2 (2011) 3–10.

Bianchi, Suzanne; Lesnard, Laurent, Nazio, Tiziana & Raley, Sara (2014). "Gender and Time Allocation in Cohabiting and Married Women and Men in France, Italy, and United States." *Demographic Research* 8 (2014) 183–216.

Booth, Alan, Crouter, Ann C., and Clements, Mari (ed.). *Couples in Conflict*. Mahwah, NJ.: Lawrence Erlbaum Associates, 2001.

Bowlby, John. *A Secure Base: Parent-Child Attachment and Healthy Human Development*. London: Routledge, 1988.

Bowlby . John. *attachment and loss*. Vol. 1. Second edition. New york, NY.: basic books, 1982.

Bowlby, John. "Maternal Care and Mental Health." *World Health Organization Monograph* (Serial No. 2), 1951.

Bretherton, Inge. "The Origins of Attachment Theory: John Bowlby and Mary Ainsworth." *Developmental Psychology* 28 (1992): 759–775.

Bryman, Alan. *Social Research Methods*. Second Edition. New York, NY.: Oxford University Press, 2004.

Bumpass, Larry and Lu, Hsien-Hen. "Trends in Cohabitation and Implication for Children Family Contexts in the United States." *Population Studies* 54:1 (2000) pp. 29–41.

Bumpass, Sweet and Cherlin, "The Role of Cohabitation in Declining Rates Marriage" *Journal of Marriage and the Family* 53 (1991) 913–927.

Chitando, Ezra and Chirongoma, Sophia. "Introduction: Justice not Silence." In *Justice not Silence: Churches facing Sexual and Gender-Based Violence*. Edited by Chitando, Ezra and Chirongoma, Sophia, 9–16. Stellenbosch: Sun Press, 2013.

Cohen, Lous, Morrison, Keith and Manion, Lawrence. *Research Method in Education*. Sixth Edition. New York, NY.: Routledge, 2007.

Corbetta, Piergiorgio, *Social Research: Theory, Methods and Techniques*. London: Sage, 2003.

Cresswell John.W. *Research Design Qualitative Quantitative and Mixed Methods Approaches*. Fourth Edition. Thousand Oaks, CA.: Sage, 2011.

Bibliography

Creswell, John W. *Education Research: Planning, Conducting and Evaluating Quantitative and Qualitative Research.* Third Edition. Boston, MA.: Pearson Education, 2012.

Creswell, John W. *Research Design: Qualitative, Quantitative and Mixed Methods Approaches.* Fourth Edition. London: Sage, 2014.

Di Gulio, Paola and Rosian, Alessandro. "Integrational Family Ties and the Diffusion of Cohabitation in Italy." *Demographic Research* 14 (2007) 441–468.

Denscombe, Martyn. *The Good Research Guide for Small Scale Social Research Projects.* Third Edition. New York, NY.: McGraw Hill, 1998.

EAC/AMREF Lake Victoria (EALP) Programme. "Addressing Mobility, Vulnerability, and Gaps in Integrated Response to HIV & AIDS in the Lake Victoria Basin." HIV Sero-behavioral Study in Six Universities in Tanzania. Final Report, 2010.

Elizabeth, Vivienne. "Cohabitation Marriage and the Unruly Consequence of Difference." *Gender and Society* 14:1 (2000) 87–110.

Eriksen, John. "Unmarried Cohabitation and Family Policy in Norway." *International Review of Sociology* 11:1 (2001) 63–74.

Finer, Lawrence B., Darroch, Jacqueline E. and Singh, Susheela. "Sexual Partnership Patterns as a Behavioral Risk Factor for Sexually Transmitted Diseases." *Perspectives on Sexual and Reproductive Health: A Journal of Peer-Reviewed Research* 31:5 (1999) 228–236. Online at DOI: https://doi.org/10.1363/3122899 [Accesses 30 October 2017].

Finer, Lawrence B. and Zolna, Mia R. "Shifts in Intended and Unintended Pregnancies in the United States, 2001–2008." *American Journal of Public Health* 104:51 (2014) 543–548.

Gabrielli, Giuseppe and Vignoli, Daniele (2012). "Breaking-Down of Marriage in Italy: Trends and Trendsetters." *Working Paper 2012/01.* Università Degli Studi di Firenze.

Giangreco, Michael F. and Taylor, Stephen J. "'Scientifically Based Research' and Qualitative Inquiry." *Research and Practice for Persons with Severe Disabilities* 28:3 (2003) 133–137.

Granviningen, Kirsten., Mitchell, R. Kirstin, Wellings, Kaye., Johnson, Anne. M., Jones, Geary, Rebecca. et al. "Reported Reasons for Breakdown of Marriage and Cohabitation in Britain: Findings from the Third National Survey of Sexual Attitudes and Lifestyles (Natsal-3)." *PLoS ONE* 12:3 (2017): e0174129. doi:10.1371/journal.pone.0174129. [Retrieved 15 September 2017].

Grinberg, Alice, Hart, Carl L., Shapiro, Jack, Keith, Diana, Taha, Farah, McNeil, Michael P., Goodwin, Renee. "Hookah Use among College Students: Prevalence, Mental Health, and Drug Use." *Drug and Alcohol Dependence* 146 (2015) 118–201.

Gold, Joshua M. "Typologies of Cohabitation: Implication for Clinical Practice and Research." *The Family Journal: Counseling and Therapy for Couples and Families* 20:3 (2012) 315–321.

Bibliography

Greenberg Jerrold S; Bruess, Clint E. and Conklin, Sarah C. *Exploring the Dimension of Human Sexuality.* Third Edition. London: Jones and Bortlett, 2007.

Hadari, Joy Moses. "Effects of Students Cohabitation in Tertiary Institutions." Daily Trust Newspaper Sunday, 2014. Online at https://www.dailytrust.com.ng/daily/education/20661-effects-of-students-cohabiting-in-tertiary-institutions [Retrieved 08 September, 2017].

Hanasono, Lisa K. and Nadler, Lawrence B. "A Dialectical Approach to Rethinking Roommate Relationship." *Journal of College Student Development* 53:5 (2012) 623–635.

Hennon, Charles B. "Conflict Management within Cohabitation Relationships." *Alternative Lifestyles* 4:4 (1981) 467–486.

Howard, Lahoma J. "Not Married, but not Single—Contrasting the Socio-Economic Experience of Cohabiting College Students with Single, Divorced and Married Students." Unpublished Paper. Santa Fe Community College, 2005.

Jonker, Jan and Pennink, Bartjan. *The Essence of Research Methodology: A Concise Guide for Master and PhD Students in Management Science.* Heidelberg: Springer, 2010.

Kheswa, G.J. and Hoho, V.N. "Exploring the Factors and Effects of Alcohol abuse on the Behaviour of University Female Students at One South African University Campus." *Rupkatha Journal on Interdisciplinary Studies in Humanities* IX:1 (2017) 291–300.

Kiernan, K.E. *Cohabitation in Klesten Europe: Trends, Issues and Implications.* Hillside, Ns.: Erbium, 2002.

Kojima, H. "Demographic Implications of increased Unmarried Cohabitation in Western Countries." *Jinko Mondai Kenkyu* 166 (1988) 52–57.

Kombo, K. and Tromp, D. *Proposal and Thesis Writing.* Nairobi: Paulines Publication African, 2006.

Kothari,C.R. *Research Methodology Methods and Methodology.* Second Edition. New Age International, 2004.

Koul lokesh M. *Methodology of Educational Research.* Third Edition. New Delhi: Vikas, 2003.

Kulu, Hill and Boyle, Paul J. "Premarital Cohabitation and Divorce: Support for the 'Trial Marriage' Theory." *Demographic Research* 23:31 (2010) 879–904.

Kumar, Ranjit. *Research Methodology a Step by Step Guide for Beginners.* Third Edition. New Delhi: Sage, 2011.

Leyaro, Vincent, Selaya, Pablo and Trifkovik, Neda. "Culture of Violence against Women: Evidence from a Field Experiment in Tanzania." Growth and Development Research Project, 07 May 2017. Online at http://economics.handels.gu.se/digitalAssets/1643/1643719_89.-trifkovic-culture-of-violence-against.pdf [Accessed on 30 October, 2017].

Mabuwa, Rumbi. *Seeking Protection: Addressing Sexual and Domestic Violence in Tanzania'a Refugee Camps.* New York, NY.: Human Rights Watch, 2000.

Bibliography

Machi, Lawrence A. and Brenda T. McEvoy. *The Literature Review.* Thousand Oaks,California: Corwin, 2009.

Maconochie, Lynne Marie; MacPherson, Diane M. and Racca, Jessica (2002) "Perceptions of Cohabitation Among College Students: Questions For the New Millenium," *FSU Journal of Behavioral Sciences* 5:1 (2002). Online at: http://digitalcommons.framingham.edu/journal_of_behavioral_sciences/vol5/iss1/3 [Accessed 31 October 2017].

Mashau, Thinandavha D. "Cohabitation and Premarital Sex Amongst Christian Youths in South Africa Today: A Missional Reflection." *HTS Teologiese Studies/Theological Studies* 67:2 (2011), Online Doi:10.4102/hts.v67i2.899 [Accessed 28 September 2017).

Matete, Rose. "Teaching Professionalism in an Accountability Age in Tanzania." *International Journal of Science and Technology* 5:2 (2016) 60–70.

Martin, Todd Forrest. "Exploring the Cohabitation Effect: Untangling the Life Course Diversity of Cohabiting Unions." PhD (Sociology) Thesis, University of British Columbia, 2013.

Mbeya Region Socio-Economic Profile. The Planning Commissioner Dar-Es-Saalam &Regional Commissioner's Office Mbeya, 1997. Ministry of Education. HIV/AIDS Policy, Dear es Salaam, 2014.

Miller, Amanda J. "Cohabiting Men's Preferences for and Roles in Determining the Outcomes of Unexpected Pregnancies." *Sociological Forum* 27:3 (2012) 708–731.

Mligo, Elia Shabani. *Introduction to Research Methodology and Report Writing. A Practical Guide for Students and Researchers in Social Sciences and the Humanities.* Eugene, Oregon: Wipf and Stock/Resource, 2016.

Mlyakado, Budeba P. and Timothy, Neema. "Effects of Students' Sexual Relationship on Academic Performance among Secondary Students in Tanzania." *Academic Research International* 5:4 (2014) 278–286.

Modebelu, Ndidi M. and Chinyere, Agommuoh P. "Environmental Hazards and Hostel Accommodation Problem Challenges for University Education in Nigeria." *US-China Education Review* 4:6 (2014) 357–367.

Muriithi-Kabaria, Joan Nduta. "Factors that Contribute to the Prevalence and Practice of Cohabitation among Kenyatta University Students, Nairobi, Kenya." M.Sc. (Family and Consumer Sciences) Thesis, Kenyatta University, Nairobi Kenya, 2006.

Mustapha, Mulikat Ladi, Odebode, Aminat Odeola, and Adegboyega, Lateef Omotosho. "Impact of Premarital Cohabitation on Marital Stability as expressed by Married Adults in Ilorin, Nigeria." *Asia Pacific Journal of Multidisciplinary Research* 5:1 (2017) 112–121.

Mwamwenda, Tuntufye Selemani. "University Students' Knowledge of HIV/AIDS at an Adventist University in Tanzania." *Mediterranean Journal of Social Sciences* 5:27 (2014) 816–820.

Mynarska, Monica and Bernardi, Laura. "Meanings and attitudes attached to Cohabitation in Poland: Qualitative analyses of the Slow Diffusion of Cohabitation among the Young Generation." *Demographic Study* 16:17 (2007) 519–554.

Bibliography

Nabors, Erin L. "Relationship Violence among College Students: The Predictive Power of Sociodemographic Characteristics and Domestic Violence Beliefs." M.A (Sociology), Orlado, Florida: University of Central Florida, 2006.

Neuman, Lawrence W. *Basics of Social Research: Qualitative and Quantitative Approaches.* Boston, MA.: Pearson, 2007.

Nimako, Simon Gyasi and Bondinuba Francis Kwesi. "An Empirical Evaluation of Student Accommodation Quality in Higher Education." *European Journal of Business and Social Sciences* 1:12 (2013) 164–177.

Nyange, Tatu M., Sikira, Anna N., Macha, Joyce G. Lymo. "Gender Based Violence and Legal Aid Services Interventions among Rural Women in Morogoro Rural and Kongwa Districts, Tanzania." *International Journal of Asian Social Science* 6:8 (2016) 446–461.

Ogolsky, Brian G., Lloyd, Sally A. and Cate, Rodney M. *The Developmental Course of Romantic Relationships.* New York, NY.: Routledge, 2013.

Ogunsula, O.M. "Premarital Behavior and Length of Courtship as a Determinant of Marital Stability among Couples Nigeria." Unpublished M.Ed. Thesis, University of Ibadan Nigeria, 2004.

Ojewola, F.O., and Akinduyo, T.E. "Prevalence and Factors Responsible for Cohabitation among Undergraduates of Adekunle Ajasin University, Ondo State, Nigeria." *American Journal of Educational Research* 5:6 (2017) 650–654.

Osuafor, Godswill N. and Ayiga, Natal. "Risky Sexual Behaviour Among Married and Cohabiting Women and its Implication for Sexually Transmitted Infections in Mahikeng, South Africa." *Sexuality and Culture* 20:4 (2016) 805–823.

Owano, Dan Abongo. "Perception of Secondary School Students on Effects of Parenting Styles on Their Academic Performance: A Case of Rongo Division, Rongo District, Kenya." Master of Education in Guidance and Counseling. Egerton University Kenya, 2010.

David, Matthew & Sutton, Carole D. *Social Research: The Basics.* London: Sage, 2004.

Pal, Saurabh and Chaurasia, Vikas. "Performance Analysis of Students Consuming Alcohol Using Data Mining Techniques." (June 23, 2017). *International Journal of Advance Research in Science and Engineering* 6:2 (2017) 238–250. Available online at SSRN: https://ssrn.com/abstract=2991748 [Accessed 31 October 2017].

Pham, Chung, Keenan, Tracy and Han, Bing. "Evaluating Impacts of Early Adolescent Romance in High School on Academic Outcomes." *Journal of Applied Economics and Business Research* 3:1 (2013) 14–33.

Posel, Dorrit. and Rudwick Stephanie (2013). "Changing Patterns of Marriage and Cohabitation in South Afrca." *Acta Juridica* 13 (2013) 169–180.

Pratto, Felicia, Sidanius, Jim and Levin, Shana. "Social Dominance Theory and the Dynamics of Intergroup Relations: Taking Stock and Looking Forward." *European Review of Social Psychology* 17 (2006) 271–320.

Bibliography

Pulerwitz, Julie, Izazola-Licea, Jose-Antonio, and Gortmaker, Steven L. "Extrarelational Sex among Mexican Men and Their Partners' Risk of HIV and other Sexually Transmitted Diseases." *American Journal of Public Health*, 91:10 (2001) 1650–1652. Online at http://dx.doi.org/10.2105/AJPH.91.10.1650 [Accessed 30 October 2017].

Risman, Barbara J., Hill, Charles T., Rubin, Zick, and Peplau, Letitia Anne. (1981). "Living together in College: Implications for Courtship." *Journal of Marriage and the Family* 43:1 (1981) 77–83.

Schaefer, Richard T. *Sociology: A Brief Introduction*. Eighth Edition. New York, NY.: McGraw Hill, 2003.

Schmidt, Haley B. "Cohabitation and Attachment Theory: Analysis of College Students." Poster Presented at Salisbury University Student Research Conference, Salisbury, Maryland, April 27, 2012. Online at http://faculty.salisbury.edu/~lcgarmon/Cohabitation_and_Attachment_Theory%20SUSRC2012.pdf [Retrieved 16 September, 2017].

Seabi, Agness Tshidi. "Marriage, Cohabitation and Domestic Violence in Mpumalaga." Magister Societatis Scientae Thesis, University of Pretoria, 2009.

Singh, Susheela and Samara, Renee. "Early Marriage among Women in Developing Countries." *International Family Planning Perspectives* 22 (1996) 148–157.

Soboyejo, "Perception of Students on Cohabitation among Undergraduates in Selected Higher Institutions in Ogun State." Master Thesis, Home Science and Management, Federal University of Agriculture, Abeokuta, Nigeria.

Smock Pamela., Gasper, Lynne M.; and Wyse, Jessica. "Nonmarital Cohabitation: Current Knowledge and Future Directions for Research." *Population Studies Center Report* No.08–648. July 2008. University of Michigan Institute for Social Research.

Smock, Pamela, Gasper, Lynne and Wyse, Jessica. *Heterosexual Cohabitation in the United State: Motives of Living Together among Young Men and Women.* Institute for Social Research, University of Michigan, 2006.

Spio-Kwofie, Adelaide, Anyobodeh, Rosemund and Abban, Godreich. "An Assessment of the Accommodation Challenges faced by Students of Tokoradi Politechnic." *International Journal of Novel Research in Marketing Management and Economics* 3:1 (2016) 64–72.

Suzuki, Kayo. "What Leads Young Adults to Cohabitation? The Effects of Family Status." M.A. (Sociology) Thesis, University of North Carolina, USA., 2006.

Swodziwa, Matthew and Kurete, Faith. "Cohabitation among Tertiary Education Students: An Exploratory Study in Bulawayo." *De Gruyter Open* vi:1 (2017) 138–148.

Tavares, Beatriz Franck, Béria, Jorge Umberto, and de Lima, Maurício Silva. "Factors associated with Drug Use among Adolescent Students in Southern Brazil." *Rev Saúde Pública* 38:6 (2004) 1–9.

Bibliography

Teachman, Jay. "Childhood Living Arrangement and the Formation of Co residential Union."*Journal of Marriage and Family* 63 (2003) 507–524.

Teachman, Jay. "Premarital Sex, Premarital Cohabitation, and the Risk of Subsequent Marital Dissolution among Women." *Journal of Marriage and Family* 65 (2003) 444–455.

Thornton, Arland, Axinn, William G. and Xie, Yu. *Marriage and Cohabitation.* Chicago, IL.: The University of Chicago Press, 2007.

Timothy, Neema. "The Influence of Sexual Activity on the Academic Performance of Students in Secondary Schools and Universities in Dar es Salaam City, Tanzania: The Case of Kinondoni District." M.A. (Demography) Thesis. University of Dar es Salaam, Tanzania, 2010.

URT. *National Higher Education Policy.* Dar es Salaam, Tanzania, 1999.

URT. *National Youth Development Policy.* Ministry of Labour, Employment and Youth Development. Dar-es-Saalam, Tanzania, 2007.

URT. National Policy on HIV/AIDS. Dar-es-Saalam, Tanzania, 2001.

Van der Lippe, Tanja, Voorpostel, Marieke and Hewitt, Belinda. "Disagreements among Cohabiting and Married Couples in 22 European Countries." *Demorgraphic Research* 31 (2014) 248–274. Online at http://www.demographic-research.org/Volumes/Vol31/10/ DOI:10.4054/Dem Res.201431.10 [Accessed 30 October 2017].

Voigt, Erick P. "Reconsidering the Mythical Advantages of Cohabitation: Why Marriage is more efficient than Cohabitation." *Indiana Law Journal* 78:3 (2003) 1069–1100. Available at: http://www.repository.law.indiana.edu/ilj/vol78/iss3/5 [Accessed 20 August 2017].

Waggoner, Lawrence W. "Marriage is on the Decline and Cohabitation is on the Rise: At What Point, if Ever, should Unmarried Partners acquire Marital Rights?" *Family Law Quarterly* 50:2 (2016) 215–246.

Wubs, Annegreet G., Aarø, Leif E., Flisher, Alan J., Bastien, Sheri, Onya, Hans E., Kaaya, Sylvia and Mathews, Catherine. "Dating Violence among School Students in Tanzania and South Africa: Prevalence and Socio-Demographic Variations." *Scandinavian Journal of Public Health* 37 (2009) 75–86.

www.ingramcontent.com/pod-product-compliance
Lightning Source LLC
Chambersburg PA
CBHW051701090426
42736CB00013B/2483